ARCHITECTURAL DESIGN

EDITORIAL OFFICES:
42 LEINSTER GARDENS, LONDON W2 3AN
TEL: 0171-402 2141 FAX: 0171-723 9540

EDITOR: Maggie Toy
EDITORIAL TEAM: Iona Baird, Stephen Watt,
Cristina Fontoura
ART EDITOR: Andrea Bettella
CHIEF DESIGNER: Mario Bettella
DESIGNER: Steven Roberts

CONSULTANTS: Catherine Cooke, Terry
Farrell, Kenneth Frampton, Charles Jencks,
Heinrich Klotz, Leon Krier, Robert Maxwell,
Demetri Porphyrios, Kenneth Powell, Colin
Rowe, Derek Walker

SUBSCRIPTION OFFICES:
UK: VCH PUBLISHERS (UK) LTD
8 WELLINGTON COURT, WELLINGTON STREET
CAMBRIDGE CB1 1HZ
TEL: (01223) 321111 FAX: (01223) 313321

USA AND CANADA: VCH PUBLISHERS INC
303 NW 12TH AVENUE DEERFIELD BEACH,
FLORIDA 33442-1788 USA
TEL: (305) 428-5566 / (800) 367-8249
FAX: (305) 428-8201

ALL OTHER COUNTRIES:
VCH VERLAGSGESELLSCHAFT MBH
BOSCHSTRASSE 12, POSTFACH 101161
69451 WEINHEIM
FEDERAL REPUBLIC OF GERMANY
TEL: 06201 606 148 FAX: 06201 606 184

Architectural Design is published six times per year (Jan/Feb; Mar/
Apr; May/Jun; Jul/Aug; Sept/Oct; and Nov/Dec).Subscription rates for
1996 (incl p&p): Annual subscription price: UK only £68.00, World DM
195, USA $142.00 for regular subscribers. Student rate: UK only
£50.00, World DM 156, USA $105.00 incl postage and handling
charges. Individual issues: £16.95/DM 42.50 (plus £2.40/DM 6 for
p&p, per issue ordered), US $28.95 (incl p&p).
For the USA and Canada, Architectural Design is distributed by
VCH Publishers Inc, 303 NW 12th Avenue, Deerfield Beach, FL
33442-1788; Telefax (305) 428-8201, Telephone (305) 428-5566 or
(800) 367-8249. Application to mail at second-class postage rates is
pending at Deerfield Beach, FL. POSTMASTER. Send address changes
to Architectural Design, 303 NW 12th Avenue, Deerfield Beach, FL
33442-1788. Printed in Italy.Origination by Media 2000, London.
All prices are subject to change without notice. [ISSN: 0003-8504]

CONTENTS

ARCHITECTURAL DESIGN **MAGAZINE**

Chalgrove Bridge, the world's
first concrete bridge with
plastic reinforcement

ARCHITECTURAL DESIGN **PROFILE** No 119

BEYOND THE REVOLUTION

Stalin's skyscraper,
Kudrinskaya, north front,
1994

Milan Sosteric, Vlaska Drug
Store, Zagreb, Croatia.
Drawing by Branka Kaminski

GUY BATTLE AND CHRISTOPHER McCARTHY

MULTI-SOURCE SYNTHESIS

Structural Substance of Composite Detailing

The iron bridge of Coalbrookedale was detailed as though it was made of timber, whilst today we see composite materials detailed as though they were steel. At present, the possibilities of detailing in composites have been unexplored, with the result that the structural form of composite construction is often bland, and fails to express the qualities of the material or the technical achievement. How we detail these composite connections is one of the essential challenges confronting structural engineers and architects today. The aim of this article is to explore methods by which details of structural significance may be developed.

Visual literacy

The understanding of architecture, and the excitement that can be generated by structure relies on visual literacy, itself based on codes and associations which vary across the globe. The modern visual literacy of structural form is now highly developed; we know that the strength and stiffness of a structural section does not depend upon the mass of the section, but on the effectiveness of its visual shape to transmit stress. An 'I' will always be stronger and stiffer than an 'H', whatever the material.

However, visual decoding is much more complex when the viewer is confronted by the numerous plates of Naum Gabo's *Head No 2*, as reading such a work requires a fundamental and fluent understanding of visual structural language, as well as an appreciation of the wealth of the symbolic vocabulary.

Despite initial preconceptions, structural engineering is not so different from sculpture, as both are ways of understanding reality. The main difference is not so much in the aims but the method. The engineer depends upon measurement and mathematical formulae to explain phenomena, whereas sculpture tends to be an intuitive and visual approach. Even these distinctions are not absolute: many a great engineer has worked intuitively and numerous sculptors have shown a rigorous intellectual approach in their work.

Structural substance

Whether we are looking at the creations of engineers or sculptors, we must be aware of the visual language; light, shape, colour, texture, lines, patterns, similarities, contrasts and movements. In engineering, visual literacy may be defined as the competence to illustrate structural substance by complementing physical function with a visual expression.

	Structural function	Visual function
Purpose	Support, enclose, contain, shelter, shield	Communicate information, express idea or attitude, convey feeling or mood, personality
Contexts	Loadings, allowable stress and strain, stability, technology, economy, culture, climate	Spatial, perceptual, environment, cultural, social expectations
Materials	Earth, stone, metal, wood, concrete, glass, plastic, fabric	Visible spectrum
Elements	Slab, panel, beam, girder, joists, column, post, tie, strut	Thick, thin, bold, slender, stiff, flexible
Attributes	Size, weight, shape, strength, stiffness, cost, durability	Position, direction, brightness, size, shape, texture, colour, surface, quality, duration
System	Arch, vault, shell, dome truss, frame, membrane	Proximity, closure, similarity, continuance, rhythm, movement
Joints	Bearing, friction, weld, cement, rivet, bolt, pin, mortar, adhesive, node	Harmony, chaos, identify similarity, contrast, ambiguity
Criteria	Equilibrium, safety, durability, economy	Composition, legibility, expressiveness, coherence, order, balance, equilibrium, mobility

Contemporary techniques for expressing structural substance

The common denominator of structural and visual function is the ordering of materials within a consistent form. A structural form

2

3

1 *Amédee Bertault*, Auguste Rodin's Hand ; *engineering and sculpture creating form out of formless matter*
2 *Cast iron detailed like timber, Coalbrookedale Bridge*
3 *Naum Gabo*, Head No 2

4

5

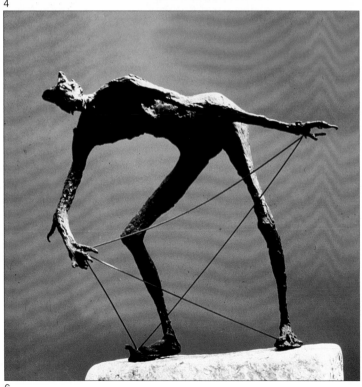

6

7

IV

devolved solely from rational assessment, without passion and sensitivity, is only a topographical solution to a technical problem; whilst a structural form developed from emotional responses, without any real root in technology, will only be an isolated graph of an individual state of mind. Structural substance requires both, and there are basic principles that relate to a sculpture or to engineering:

Structure	Composition in space
Unity	Complete vision
Consistency	Clarity of expression

Admittedly, instruction about the techniques associated with sculpture – symbolising stability or movement – may seem out of context with the design of modern structural engineering, and the freedoms associated with sculpture may seem incompatible with the formulated disciplines of traditional structural design. Nevertheless, there are some design criteria associated with both the work of sculptors and engineers which assist in illustrating structural.

The suggestive power of structural substance of composite materials

Our eye senses not only colour but also data, which enables the brain to form images of the three-dimensional spatial characteristic of objects, allowing sensory judgement of symbolic content. We react primarily to:

Proportions	Dimensions of elements
Composition	The space between the elements
Contrast	The relationship between the elements (curves and straight lines)

In developing a detail in composites we understand its functional purpose, but it is much more difficult to define the emotional and spiritual aspects of its structural substance. We should once again involve ourselves in the 'Drama of Engineering', in its range from creating a secure enclosure with reassuring interlocking arches, to the uninhabitable projection of angular forms. Detailing in composites offers the opportunity of creating an appearance of a personality appropriate to its purpose and significance.

Composite form and detailing with symbolised harmony

The word harmony may be defined as a state of order, implying something which is aesthetically pleasing or visually stable, and is derived from the Greek work *harmos*, meaning a joint, and *harmozein*, to join together. With composites, we are involved in the physical and visual joining together of structural elements, such as beams, columns, ties and struts, with pins, knots and stitching. In as much as we are capable of assessing musical harmony instinctively, it may be possible to train our eyes to

10

11

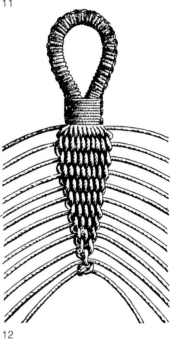
12

8

9

The theme of the human torso is one of the most frequent means of symbolising stability or movement
4, 5 The form of The Thinker *by Rodin has been developed to contain an inner force, whereas the iron connection of Brighton Pier clasps the forces between intercepting elements*
6, 7 The diagonal ties held by Richier's Devil with Claws *create forces in as much as the bracing at the Pompidou Centre accommodates them*
8, 9 The two angels in Lynn Chadwick's Winged Figure *represent our mechanical age in which the work bears witness to the art movement of the 60s: calculation, invention and understanding replaced the free play of the imagination, and the formal order of structural systems achieved aesthetic results – creating a constructive symbol of the aeroplane design technical revolution*
10 Interlocking elephant trunks
11 A pattern of dendrites, created by cellular automation with an asymmetric transition rule
12 Puddening an anchor ring

evaluate the visual harmonies of structures.

The presence or lack of these different aspects of structural substance reveals the professional touch of skilful detailing. They effect the overall impact of the composition, the feeling for the onlooker that everything is in its right place, that nothing could be added or taken away; the unmistakable completeness of symbolic content. Armed with these fundamental principles of form, the designer will find that he or she can see and correct many things that disturb the efficiency of the detail's geometry. A random grouping of composite elements will not produce a serviceable bridge, and neither will an unorganised collection of perceptual elements result in a coherent visual statement; only when the composite materials are properly joined and related to each other does the bridge become serviceable.

To our eyes the geometry of a bridge is seen as a complex arrangement of lines, shapes, volumes, masses, shadows and colours, which all seem incidental to the detail itself, yet all become a vital part in determining its value as a work of engineering. To some extent it is a good test of a 'satisfactory' detail that it composes well when seen from any direction, which means that it has the completeness of conception, as emphasised by Michelangelo in his work. Interestingly, the structural engineer Robert Maillart asserted: 'if the geometry of a structure looks right, it is right'.

There are several features which should be borne in mind when designing structure:

Simplicity: Simplicity is common to excellence in all the arts; it is elegance with economy of material. Just as in sculpture the most elegant solution may be achieved by simple gestures, the most economical solution in structural design may prove to be the best. Simplicity is not necessarily easy to achieve, as the impression of ease is usually the result of intensive skilful effort.

Necessity: Necessity is perhaps the key to harmony. How magnificent is the result if there is nothing in a detail, but that which is necessary. This is not a paradox. The mind is at rest in the acceptance of necessity, but is uneasy with the superfluous, the factitious.

Order: The principle of order is to avoid unnecessary accessories. The geometry should be so refined that one can neither remove nor add any element without disturbing the harmony of the whole. Order means clarity. Geometry with too many directions creates disquiet, confuses the observer and arouses disagreeable emotions; good order is achieved by limiting the directions of geometrical lines and edges.

We can also include the repetition of equal elements under the role of order. Repetition provides rhythm, which creates satisfaction. Yet too much repetition leads to monotony, so often encountered in 20th-century structures. The designer should interrupt its predictability and introduce some element of surprise.

The appropriate details of a composite connection are enhanced by the harmonies of simplicity, necessity and order; but the creation of originality requires tension between variety and similarity, and between complexity and order, which doubtlessly demands artistic skills. Designers should take note of the works of past and present sculptors who have been able to achieve fluidity, as well as the unexpected, within the order of a harmonious design.

Summary

Detailing of composite materials frequently lacks flair and imagination, failing to illustrate the qualities inherent in the material or the skill of their authors. The product is often merely a statement of the facts, unable to invoke the excitement, expectations, interest and even the admiration of craftsmanship.

Remember the delight, when as a child you built your first structure? To come near to this fundamental awareness of art, you need to sense and feel for a structural symbolic context, in terms of lines shapes, forms and colours. Like the Chinese artist of old, say a prayer and learn to be humble before the pencil touches the paper.

The authors would like acknowledge the contribution made by Douglas Broadley to the preparation of this article.

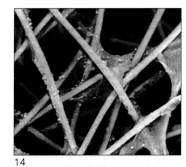

14

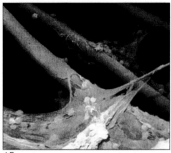

15

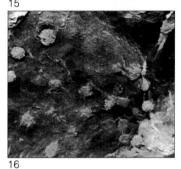

16

13 *Sketch development of a composite bridge*
14, 15, 16 *Scaffolding has been constructed to provide a template for formation of new tissue (shown enlarged, from above to below, x200, x500, x1000). The biodegradable plastic has been seeded with cells, which divide and assemble until they cover most of the structure. Eventually the plastic degrades leaving only tissue.*

STALIN'S SKYSCRAPER

RONAN THOMAS

Standing at the crossroads between Krasnsaya Presnya and Sadovaya Kudrinskaya, in northwest Moscow, is a monumental anachronism to an era passing uneasily yet rapidly into history. Rising to over 500 feet and surmounted by a gleaming copper spire it gazes down from a commanding position onto the Moscow city skyline. The apartment building at Kudrinskaya Square bestrides Moscow's central road artery, the Garden Ring, as an ageing Stalinist colossus, arguably the finest example of an architectural school which embodied the cumulative ideals of the Soviet State.

In the late 40s, the Soviet Union was still recovering from the catastrophic human and material losses suffered in the Great Patriotic War against Germany. In this aftermath, day to day life in Moscow, outside whose gates the German advance had been halted in 1942, the average citizen was subjected to severe overcrowding, with rooms frequently partitioned by blankets. Against this background of personal discomfiture, Stalin ordered construction of a series of grandiloquent buildings designed to accommodate the elite of Soviet society, and in January 1947, the government received instructions for these new high-rise buildings.

They were to stand apart from other city buildings by virtue of their exceptional expressiveness, unique architecture, picturesque style, unprecedented size and visual power. In sum, they were to provide the centrepiece of entirely new architectural ensembles and to reinvigorate the war damaged capital. They were to form the show-piece of Stalin's new Socialist Realist, city skyline.

The building scheme was launched to great fanfare, and a leading Moscow evening newspaper enthused about the new form of skyscraper, 'Standing majestically triumphant over the world and glittering with the beckoning lights of red stars'. The Chairman of the State Architecture Committee, G Simonov, noted in *Culture and Life* and *Pravda* that:

> Moscow's skyscrapers will be an advanced and progressive architecture based on rich national traditions drastically different from the soulless and formalistic creations of modern bourgeois architects.

Official Soviet opinion not only eulogised the architectural splendours of these new high-

rises, but also contrasted the 'purity' of their construction with the oppressiveness of American skyscrapers, depicted conversely as constructs designed to exploit the proletariat.

Since the 30s, Stalin had visualised a new city skyline, with buildings spread evenly across the city, providing a natural transition from Moscow's highest planned point, its so-called composition axis. On this axis a Palace of Soviets was to be constructed, a mammoth multi-tier tower topped by a statue of Lenin. The palace, planned in 1933, was never built but its counterpoints, the skyscraper series, remain as Stalin's architectural legacy.

The construction of the apartment block took place against a backdrop of concerted economic reconstruction and political ruthlessness in the Soviet Union. The fourth Five Year Plan, launched in 1946, fell far short of its promised benefits nationally, but was succeessful in reducing food prices and restoring national wage levels. The Central Committee of the Soviet Communist Party (CPSU), which had played a rather minor role during the war, was revamped and reorganised in the period up to 1952 and became an increasingly important organ of state, particularly in its Draconian legislation of art, architecture and literature. Considering that this was the era of mass deportation of political and social undesirables to Siberia, its grip over cultural life was absolute.

In wider society, Stalin was reasserting his control over Soviet citizens in almost every sphere of life after a period of temporary abatement caused by the expedient of defeating the Germans during the war. Prominent literary and cultural figures were subject to strict censure and, frequently, imprisonment. Repression of this nature was exemplified in the architectural styles enforced on the architects of the new apartment blocks and ministries. Officially, these new buildings were to be accessible to ordinary citizens – 'socialist in content and national in form, close to every Soviet citizen and every worker'. In reality, they were designed for the elite, and, even more importantly, their design reflected Stalin's preference towards monumental constructions.

Stalin, like Hitler, had once been a choirboy, and retained a fondness for the spirit of cathedral construction, particularly in the case of impressive spires. All seven planned skyscrapers in Moscow, including Kudrinskaya, were to carry spires atop their central towers. The architects of the Soviet Ministry of Foreign Affairs, Vladimir Gelfreich and Mikhail Minkus, initially neglected to include a spire in their architectural plans, favouring instead a flat steel roof. When visiting the construction site, Stalin is reported to have noticed its absence and to have muttered the single angry word 'spire' to the architects as he left, and the design was immediately changed.

It was not by chance that these more traditional features of old Russian architecture were reflected in the construction of the 50s. During and after the war, the CPSU, encouraged by Stalin, drew on national Russian ideas, marking the turn of the Soviet state from the ideology of internationalism, professed in the 20s and 30s, to the idea of imperialism. The culture and art of the period witnessed a shift to traditional Russian themes, forms and pre-revolutionary decorative styles. This was evident in the introduction of new military decorations for the Red Army based on historical Russian figures, and a shift in official Soviet attitudes towards the Russian orthodox church, from the hatred of the 30s to reconciliation.

The Kudrinskaya Square project was developed by two famous Soviet architects, both recipients of the Stalin Award and members of the Soviet Academy of Architecture – Mikhail Posokhin (1909-89) and Asot Mndoyants (1909/ 10-1966). They were supported in these gargantuan developments by chief constructor Mikhail Vokhomsky, and a team of 13 other architects and engineers from 1948. Sculptures and reliefs decorating the building were made by three other famous Russian architects, N Nikogosyan, M Anikushin and M Baburin, whilst specific interior designs were carried out by Russian painter Pavel Korin; chosen for his expertise in traditional forms of decoration and as a noted restorer of icons praising old Russia.

The purpose of this building was ideological, demonstrating the power, beauty and grandeur of the Soviet State, and 'leading all peoples fighting for peace, freedom and democracy towards the victory of communism'. To this end, Kudrinskaya represented a particularly complex and uneconomical construction with much unused space; atypical for a Soviet residential block. Indeed, expert contemporary opinion felt that the building was over decorated and that the expensive materials used for its construction represented over-indulgence. However, no one was arguing with Stalin.

To construct the block at Kudrinskaya, existing settlements were razed to the ground, and the inhabitants relocated elsewhere. The neighbouring streets were widened, with the

intention of enhancing the overall effect of the building by giving it a significant approach, complete with park and tree-lined avenue.

Along with architectural features common to the other six high-rise buildings, the project included a number of architectural distinctions. Kudrinskaya Square was characterised by an exceptional number of tiers, and initially a tent roof instead of a spire to ensure a visual connection with other Moscow city buildings. All these features, especially the tent roof, were features common to old Russian architecture.

Due to the steep relief structure in the side streets, the building was erected on a huge wide base foundation, which for the first time in the practice of Soviet building, was utilised to provide residents with a cinema, hairdresser's, fashion house and four food halls, or Gastronoms.

The food halls were among the most sumptuous ever designed for a Moscow building, and were connected using interior staircases and cargo lifts. With a total area of over 5,000 square metres – approximately the area of two six-storey buildings – the food halls were finished with polished marble, granite and majolica, and at intervals, monumental concrete and alabaster reliefs were placed, depicting Soviet stars, mothers nurturing communist youth and determined soldiers brandishing sub-machine-guns.

Kudrinskaya took five years to build, using a German work-force, Wehrmacht prisoners of war retained by Stalin to act as virtual slaves in its construction. No records exist of these individuals, their fate is unknown, although the tower is now inhabited by many expatriates.

By 1954 the building was ready to begin its official and residential responsibilities, and was presented to the Ministry of Aviation, earning the nickname of the 'Pilot's House'. Apartments were reserved for senior Ministry of Aviation and Moscow Council bureaucrats as well as eminent academicians, actors, artists and the director of Moscow's Maly Theatre.

In the years following its construction the building continued as a preferred residence for the Soviet elite under successive premiers. However, following 1991 and the development of aggressive market capitalism, residency continues to confer social status although its inhabitants today would have been unthinkable when it was first built.

Over half of the building is now occupied by expatriates, Americans, British, Italians, French and Germans, many of whom are employed by larger western companies which can afford to rent apartments there at exorbitant market rates; at least as expensive as London or New York. In rooms designed for distinguished Soviet admirals, pop music blares incessantly, and television advertising proclaims the grow-

FROM ABOVE: View from the north; view upwards

ing affluence of many of Moscow's populace.

Today, the richest inhabitants of Moscow are nationals, and those living in Kudrinskaya are often real-estate brokers, renting apartments in this and other buildings, driving new BMWs and sporting Ray Ban sunglasses. They exist rather uneasily with the building's older Russian residents who more broadly reflect its past and who regard them with suspicion.

The interior of the building continues to exude a tremendous air of the late Stalinist and early Khrushchev period, combining opulence with something also rather sinister. One can readily imagine a 'midnight knock' from leather coated strangers, a rapid fall from grace and an anonymous trip to Siberia. Needless to say, the magnificence of Kudrinskaya also gives it a peculiar sense of faded charm, unlike most other places in Moscow. Its atmosphere of undoubted corruption makes it easy to visualise the 'fat cats' of Khrushchev's Kremlin luxuriating in their apartments toasting Yuri Gagarin's conquest of space whilst living standards in the Russian countryside remained in some areas at medieval levels.

Living in one of the two room apartments is to experience something of this period. Its grand interior, replete with high ceilings, carpeted walls and obligatory chandeliers, is stamped with the unerring Russian instinct to over decorate. The apartment also carries evidence of recent Soviet history. Book lined shelves, containing entire 24 volume sets of the works of Marx and Lenin, are complemented by CPSU annual periodicals which begin at 1966 but finish at 1989; as if the inhabitants of the apartment sensed that the system would not endure for much longer.

The entrance halls remain stupendous, with huge chandeliers and three massive elevators stamped with the date 1957. Of these three, only two are working at any given moment, and their slow, clanking progress upward encourages use of the stairs despite the long climb. The musty stairs frequently assail the climber with an appalling stench as he ascends, the result of faulty plumbing, but generally the building is kept immaculate by dedicated staff.

The food halls, on each corner of the building, are still by far and away the most decorative features of the building. However, they still betray the national economic fortune, and the products available to most Russians shoppers. Stocks are not constant, the somewhat surly female staff are anaemic-looking, and purchase of basic items still requires maddening recourse to an enclosed kiosk and voucher system. Queues are short but customers have no hesitation in jostling others if they hesitate over items, yet the quality of foodstuffs in these shops is improving radically.

It is from the windows of Kudrinskaya's apartments that one best appreciates the history of Moscow, and the changed environment in which the city finds itself today. Views of nearby buildings represent both the old and the new, but it is at sunset that modern Moscow asserts itself. The gaudy lights of the bridge over the Moskva river are switched on, and neon signs attract those with money to the capital's ever changing series of night-clubs. In Kudrinskaya itself, the 'Flame' cinema, built with the sole intention of showing the exemplary works of Soviet cinema, has become a seedy night club called 'The Fire Bird'. Lit Catseyes, set in the drive, beckon clubbers to the interior, and a gold Rolls-Royce Silver Spur is often seen parked ostentatiously outside.

If a building may be said to symbolise an era and an individual, then Kudrinskaya still provides a potent legacy for Joseph Stalin, the cult he built around his own personality and the ideals he espoused to a largely quiescent if not enthusiastic society. Of today's architectural aspirations and values, however, Kudrinskaya's builders would look askance. The largest and most sumptuous buildings in Moscow to be planned and constructed in recent years embody new realities in Russia. These are the various grand schemes for corporate towers, conceived by Russia's new 'robber baron' class of commercial bankers, and the glass fronted business centre on Tverskaya Street – owners McDonalds.

FROM LEFT: East entrance hall; interior corridor. All photographs by the author

Island Nation Aesthetics

Arata Isozaki

The Eyes of the Skin
Architecture and the Senses

Juhani Pallasmaa

Two Way Stretch

Robert Maxwell

The Japanese architect, Arata Isozaki is one of the most innovative and influential architects working today; creating an impressive *oeuvre*, developed over the past 35 years, and spread over many continents. Based on his lecture given at the Royal Academy in London, June 1995, this polemic presents Isozaki's view on individual island aesthetics; arguing for the creation of a singularity of purpose and design, as illustrated in Japanese culture, especially in terms of space, design and the traditional organisation of life. Isozaki defines the nature of Japan as an island, with an invisible boundary where the exterior automatically becomes the interior, and explores where the destruction of such conditions will lead its aesthetics as the Millennium approaches. This influential architect has a history and perception which will inspire the reader.

Paperback 1 85490 437 X
217 x 140 mm, 64 pages
April 1996

This much admired Finnish intellectual and architect, presents his long awaited polemical statement on the situation facing architecture today. Fresh from his successful exhibition 'Animal Architecture', the result of 18 years research examining the relationships between animals and their environs, he uses this opportunity to crystallise the theories and phenomena he has observed and developed. Using this framework Pallasmaa considers the dominating visual imagery of the Modern Movement, exploring the effects of this style over other contemporary genres.

Paperback 1 85490 439 6
217 x 140 mm, 64 pages
April 1996

In this polemic, Robert Maxwell, the renowned architectural critic, reacts against the definition of styles and ideologies, such as Hi-tech and Classical Revival, positing a more flexible mediatorial position that does not attempt to reduce the work of unique individuals into palatable fictional movements. This discussion covers the alternative approaches of abstraction, which brings a kind of personal freedom, and representation, which carries a social duty and therefore deals with the potentially conflicting demands of personal expression and the contextual forces in the environment.

Paperback 1 85490 438 8
217 x 140 mm, 64 pages
April 1996

Polemics: The new series from the Academy Group presents a forum where serious, theoretical and controversial issues can be raised and publicised, enabling world renowned architects and critics to air their views. Each book carries only one text by a respected contemporary author, and is presented in small accessible packaging. The series commences with three key architectural polemicists, Arata Isozaki, Robert Maxwell and Juhani Pallasmaa.

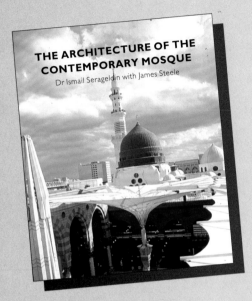

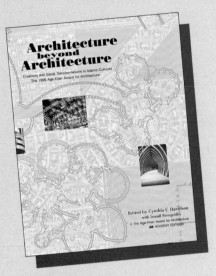

The Architecture of the Contemporary Mosque

Dr Ismaïl Serageldin with James Steele

Mosques play a central role in Muslim communities, not simply enclosing a sacred space, discrete from its secular surroundings, but also providing the power to sanctify the words and acts of the believers; the minaret, dome, gateway and calligraphy performing specific tasks within this sacred composition. Inevitably, during recent years, the orthodox role of the mosque has evolved; a process which is reflected in both its design and role within Muslim societies. This authoritative text is a unique appraisal of these architectural and sociological developments, exploring traditional and contemporary practice, within a global religious context.

Hardback 1 85490 394 2
305 x 252 mm, 192 pages
100 illustrations, 40 colour
March 1996

Architecture Beyond Architecture
The Aga Khan Award for Architecture

Edited by Cynthia C Davidson with Ismaïl Serageldin

Continuing our series on the Aga Khan Award for Architecture, this book details the twelve nominated projects. A strong critical dimension is evident in the discourse associated with this year's awards. It is reflected in this publication, allowing the jury to outline the rationale for its decisions, and their relevance to contemporary Muslim societies. While the jury's decision was unanimous, the debate surrounding the decision provides a real contribution to the critical architectural debate world-wide.

Paperback 1 85490 443 4
279 x 217 mm, 176 pages
Illustrated throughout
January 1996

Nancy Wolf

Karen A Franck

This *Art & Design Monograph* presents the work of the architectural artist, Nancy Wolf, who explores the relationship between buildings and people, asking us to reassess our preconceptions; her stunningly incisive paintings and drawings reveal how people react to the built environment. The work is discussed by the architectural lecturer Karen A Franck, who has watched this body of work develop over many years, and utilises this experience to illustrate the artist's incredible insight. The book is both aesthetically and intellectually stimulating, and includes a stunning selection of Nancy Wolf's images which highlight the much deeper sociological discussions they provoke.

Paperback 1 85490 351 9
305 x 252 mm, 120 pages
Illustrated throughout
July 1996

Further information can be obtained from Academy Group Ltd, Tel: 0171 402 2141 Fax: 0171 723 9540, or from your local sales office:
VCH Publishers, 303 NW 12th Avenue, Deerfield Beach, Florida, Tel: (305) 428 5566 / (800) 367 8249 Fax: (305) 428 8201;
VCH, Boschstrasse 12, Postfach 101161, 69451 Weinheim, Federal Republic of Germany, Tel: 06201 606 144 Fax: 06201 606 184;
VCH, 8 Wellington Court, Wellington Street, Cambridge, CR1 1H2, Tel: 01223 321111 Fax: 01223 313321

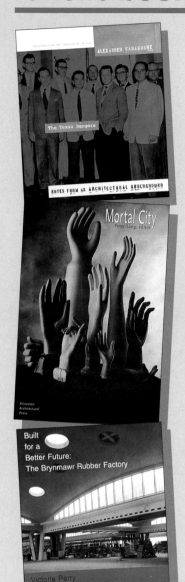

THE TEXAS RANGERS, Alexander Caragonne, MIT, 442pp, ills, HB £42.50

In 1950s America, a group of young men came to teach at the University of Texas School of Architecture in Austin. Revolutionising architectural pedagogy, the 'Texas Rangers' developed a programme that conflicted with established hierarchies, and introduced the concepts of architectural space, Gestalt psychology, the phenomenon of transparency and the architectural idea. This dimly perceived underground' is fully documented for the first time by former student Caragonne.

Concentrating largely on the charismatic figures of Colin Rowe and Bernhard Hoesli, Caragonne depicts the careers of the Texas Rangers both before and after their time at Austin, and examines their widespread influence on architectural teaching. It is argued that some 30 years after the events described here, every school in the United States has at least one or two staff members educated to think in the manner taught by these men, an effect similar to, 'turning two rabbits loose in an open wood'. Caragonne presents the impact of the group – John Hejduk, Robert Slutzky, Lee Hodgden, John Shaw and Werner Seligmann – on the American postwar educational programme in dramatic form; a dramatis personae setting the scene for what is a well-known, but little-recorded chapter in architectural teaching.

'Notes' from an architectural underground these are not; the years of the educational 'reformation' at Austin are extensively presented as lying somewhere between embryonic revolution and myth. A less subjective account may have produced a tighter script, but enthusiasm is all as Caragonne sweeps his audience through the acts of his ten-year work, with the help of personal testimonies from students, and interviews with surviving Texas Rangers. *S Parkin*

MORTAL CITY, Peter Lang, Princeton Architectural Press, 111pp, b/w ills, PB, £12.95

Urban violence increasingly dominates our day-to-day existence; we watched footage of the earthquake in Japan, the bombing of Chechnya, the war in Bosnia and not so long ago, we watched the horror of the Los Angeles riots.

Mortal City probes the nature of urban violence, the essays presenting several different approaches to the subject, reflecting the most recent historical, geographical, and theoretical developments in these fields; authors include Donald Albrecht, Lebbeus Woods and Diane Ghirardo, and there is an interview with Mark Wigley entitled 'Fear Not . . .'

This book is not a celebration of the city, but a warning light for everyone who lives and works there. Buildings in the ghettos of America grow claws and spikes, their entrances metal plates and any additional openings are sealed, cutting down on light, ventilation and the ability to escape or enter. The changes that violence has imposed on architecture are immeasurable – for example, the metal detectors at the World Trade Centre – as is the disruption of existing landscapes for new buildings – indeed building itself is by its very nature an aggressive act. We have gone from fearing the death of the city, to fearing the city of death and this traumatic change is reflected passionately in this book. The very definitions of the city and of violence are constantly being revised, and the impact of violence has moved beyond the traditional arenas of conflict to pervade daily life. *C Fontoura*

BUILT FOR A BETTER FUTURE; THE BRYNMAWR RUBBER FACTORY, Victoria Perry, White Cockade, 96pp, b/w ills, PB £12.99

The story of the Brynmawr Rubber Factory in the Welsh Borders reads like a modern fairy-tale, and in this engagingly personal book, Victoria Perry charts the progress of this spirited post-war project. A scheme which strove to bring a new manufacturing life-force to a town devastated by the decline of the coal industry. So successful was this reversal of socio-economic privation, and so impressive the nature of the architecture and its interaction with the workforce, that the factory was acknowledged by Reyner Banham as having 'one of the most impressive interiors built in Britain since St Paul's and was heralded as a modernistic symbol of the manufacturing age.

We see the building's development not only through a wide range of visual material, but also through the personalities and characters involved: the idealistic young designers of the Architects' Co-operative Partnership, the dedicated Ove Arup engineers, the baffled civil servants in Cardiff and the client, Lord 'Jim' Forrester, whose faith in the power of architecture to transform lives and rejuvenate communities spearheaded the crusade.

Sadly, this tale of human and architectural triumph has an ironic twist. Today, 50 years on, this once proud symbol of prosperity stands as a testament to economic failure; decaying, abandoned and threatened with demolition. Heated debate continues and the fate of the 'eyesore' is still being juggled between angry locals, councillors, entrepreneurs and architectural preservation groups alike. Our involvement, by this stage, is such that we too share the author's heartfelt desire that this book should not be read as the Brynmawr Rubber Factory's epitaph. *L Ryan*

THE GOTHIC REVIVAL, Kenneth Clark, John Murray, 240pp, b/w ills, PB £13.99

First published in 1928 while Clark was still at Oxford, *The Gothic Revival* has become a seminal text; the first objective appraisal of the movement and a document in the history of taste. Nothing had been written on the subject since Eastlake's *History* in 1872, and Clark was some 25 years ahead of a more general re-evaluation of Victorian architecture. He wrote at a time when its buildings were considered 'monsters, unsightly wrecks stranded on the mudflats of Victorian taste', when Modernism was taking structural rationalism to its logical conclusions and when 'extreme simplicity [was] supposed to be beyond the charge of vulgarity'. With this in mind Clark's text is remarkably circumspect. He indeed questions the pastiche of Strawberry Hill and Fonthill; the 'grubby gothic' of the commissioner's churches; the archaeological exactitude of the ecclesiologists; the horror of their and Scott's restorations; the flimsy, one-dimensional buildings of Pugin and his adoption 'of one of the most rigorous systems of taboo that have ever oppressed the inventive spirit'; but he also appreciates the movement for what it was, 'a triumph of idealism in a utilitarian age'. Clark divided the revival into two phases: the Picturesque and the Ethical. The first where the full imaginative powers and exuberance of the Gothic were realised, and the second where they were debased by the injection of archaeological exactitude and morality. To this end Clark concentrates more on the emergence of the Revival than its full flowering, and such notable figures as Street are absent. He is nevertheless 'seduced' by Pugin, who he restores to his proper position, and gives full coverage to Ruskin and Scott (the latter if only as a 'rough-and-ready symbol of the whole complicated affair'). At a time when the 'dismal', 'half-hearted . . . gabled villas of suburbia are now desirable properties and Post-Modernism is criticised for its vulgar decoration, Clark's closing line is a relevant today as it was in 1928: '"Blessed are those who have taste", said Nietzsche, "even although it be bad taste."' *R Bean*

TOKYO; A SPATIAL ANTHROPOLOGY, Jinnai Hidenobu, Univ. of California, 236pp, b/w illus, HB £32.00

This book sets out to examine the layering and development of the city of Tokyo, which is no simple feat. Attempting to show that historical structures and planning still formulate the existing heterogeneous cityscape, Jinnai draws comparisons with other capital cities, but considers that in comparison with the authentic character of New York or Venice, Tokyo has 'lost the face of its own past'. Taking a walk through the high and low cities of Edo, and showing the topographical influences of the waterways and high ground surrounding the bay, clear relation can be made between the contemporary profile and the urban fabric that existed before the natural and man-made destruction of the Great Kanto Earthquake in 1923 and World War II.

It is a delightfully illustrated monochrome book, with beautiful wood cuts and drawings, but a single criticism would be that the initial discussion of the city topology and street patterns do not have sufficient maps to elucidate these descriptions fully.

Separated into sections it initially deals with the cultural, social and topographical divisions of the city and finally the modern city and its morphology. The aspect of Tokyo Bay is discussed through its influences on the activities in the public realm, and also in the existence of urban waterways and canals providing transport through the centre of the city. The waterways were social interaction points with red-light areas, theatres and open entertainment areas predominantly occurring along the water edge. This changed in the modern period when waterfronts became built-up, and prominent buildings built next to bridges.

The book goes on to discuss the effects of modernism on the city in more recent times and concludes with suggestions for future urban planning. Originally published in 1985, in Japan, when Tokyo was developing incredibly quickly with a high turnover of property, vast redevelopments and investments, a new addendum in the English version examines the effect of the early 90s recession, on slowing the rate of expansion. *I Baird*

BIBLIOTHÈQUE NATIONALE DE FRANCE, 1989-1995, Dominique Perrault, Birkhäuser, 232pp, 240 colour, 78 b/w ills, HB £59.00

In 1989, architect, Dominique Perrault shot to fame with his winning proposal for France's latest and most ambitious grands projet, the new Bibliothèque nationale de France. As always, the winning proposal – four shimmering, L-shaped towers enclosing an immense piazza – caused the most heated of Gallic argument; for a start, the youth of the designer was deemed ignoble of this vast symbolic work in which national heritage was at stake! Never have critics been proved so wrong. The six-year project was executed flawlessly, in record time and strictly within budget. In March of this year, the Bibliotèque nationale de France – the largest and most sophisticated library in the world – was inaugurated by President Mitterrand and the nation is still oooh-là-là-ing at its most prestigious architectural asset to date.

This magnificent book pays tribute to Perrault's work in a way that lets the achievement speak for itself. Texts by François Mitterrand, Jaques Toubon, Jack Lang, Emile Biasini and Richard Rogers among many significant others, highlight the enormity of the project and the impact of its success, while insightful interviews, particularly with the architect and author himself, provide us with a more direct and intimate recollection of events, revealing the complicated nature of building a structure to house France's awesome literary heritage, while also providing a place of study, research and cultural interaction. This textual account is followed by a comprehensive visual diary of the project. Sketches, plans, models and previously unpublished colour photographs trace development from concept to completion; showing us the various stages, from the Tolbiac site as urban wasteland on the banks of the Seine, to fine interior detailing of the completed project. In addition to the incisive text and images, space is allowed for the relevant technical detail and the sparkling career of 36 year-old Dominque Perrault. *L Ryan*

THE ART OF CONSTRUCTION, Kingfisher, 46pp, illus, HB £12.99

With the exhortation to 'Touch me, feel me, sticker me, move me' as the introduction to a new interactive book for the younger reader, one could be forgiven for thinking that this English version of a successful French series might not be for the faint-hearted. *The Art of Construction*, however, takes a wonderfully quick and exciting journey through the great ages of architecture, following the developments of Ancient Egypt, Greece and Rome through to present day pyramids and modern skyscrapers. Chidren are encouraged to find the missing illustrations provided on a sheet of stickers and to pull out a large medieval castle cleverly sectioned to show construction stages, whilst an attractive semi-opaque reproduction of Frank Lloyd Wright's Falling Water may, however, be aimed at the more adult reader. The book is informative and interesting to read and any further explanation necessary is given in the comprehensive glossary of terms at the back of the book.

Aimed at readers of eight years and upwards, the book is well crafted, highly illustrated from a variety of sources, with different surfaces, cuts and folds on each page and is designed to be taken apart, quite literally. *I Baird*

THE ARCHITECTURE OF NEW PRAGUE 1895-1945, Rostislav Svacha with photographs by Jan Maly, MIT Press, pp576, b/w ills, HB £34.95

Six years on from the fall of the Communism in Czechoslovakia, and at a time when the disintegration of the former Eastern bloc states is prompting a reassessment of the avant-garde beyond the Iron Curtain, Rostislav Svacha's book, beautifully produced by MIT, is set to become the standard text on this brief but intense period of architectural activity in Prague between 1895 and 1945. Svacha seeks to document the third of the three 'great periods' in the history of Bohemian architecture, that which succeeded the late Gothic of the Middle Ages and the high baroque of the late 18th century. His approach is both scholarly and meticulous, and his style clear despite the huge amount of information conveyed. He skilfully interweaves commentaries on contemporary political and social events with his exposition of the growth of the architectural avant-garde, showing how closely cultural movements were entwined with the birth of the Modern Czech state.

In 1895 Prague had been a self-governing city for 45 years and the spirit of nationalism guided architects in their search for a modern style. First, as all over Europe, this took the form of an eclectic historicist revival, of specifically Czech precedents, an approach enshrined in Balsanek and Poliva's Municipal House which forms the background image of the book's cover: the point from which the 'New Architecture' was to depart. In 1895 the *Manifesto of the Czech Modern* ushered in this new period with its subsequent review of contemporary architecture entitled 'The Modern Style or National Direction'. Here notions of Czechoslovakia as a modern industrial nation intermingled with socialist tendencies to reject a retrograde architectural syntax and look forward to a non-imitative, socially and functionally oriented style. Svacha defines the first stage in this search as the Modern Style, first Ornamental and then Geometrical, under the influential leadership of Kotera. Gradually one sees the reduction of ornament, its transformation to symbolism (as in Bilek's remarkable villa), and the stripping down of surface and form – most elegantly realised in Novotny's Stenc building. From here architecture departed from social and political obligation to produce the brief flowering of the Czech Cubist movement, its unique œuvre cut short by the War. Following the creation of the independent Czech state, attention was firmly focused upon provision of large-scale housing, town planning and infrastructure. While Purism did develop a strong tradition, based one might say on the artistic impulse of Cubism, it was Functionalism, both Scientific and Emotional, which was to dominate the 20s and 30s.

Indeed, the original Czech title of Svacha's book – *Od moderny k funkcionalisme* – gives a clear indication of the central theme which runs through the 50 years examined: the progress of functionalism as the modern style of a country with increasing socialist leanings, from its implicit origins in Kotera's theories, to its apogee under the politically militant leadership of Tiege, to its ultimate imputation under the Soviet regime from 1945. In his article 'On New Art' in 1900, Kotera had already intimated several of the ideas which were to become central to the Functionalist doctrine – the demand for truthfulness, the need to start with the purpose of the building, with the space and its constructive expression as opposed to the facade and its decoration. By 1930 and the dawn of the Depression, Tiege had developed these theories to their extreme in his collection of essays *Contemporary International Architecture*: 'Architecture, which in our time has been given an absolutely new technology, new materials, and constructive means, and which is being challenged with tasks quite different from those it performed in the religious, feudal Middle Ages, is also being separated from the fine arts; it ceases to be an art or a decorative craft and is becoming science, technology and industry.' This extreme rationalism was applied on an urban scale in planning schemes which sought to divide the city into monofunctional zones, separating business, residential and industrial areas; in apartment buildings; and in the ultimate reductivist architectural form of the minimal dwelling – Leva fronta's L-Project taking collective living to its extreme with each apartment consisting only of a sleeping cabin and the most essential sanitary provision, every other facility being communal. As Svacha writes, 'architects took up the roles of sociologists and philosopher organisers'. Janak's Evangelical Meeting House could be described as 'a manifesto of Scientific Functionalism' and it is this building – with its clearly separated functions, its industrial shed roof and campanile – which is inset on the cover to demonstrate clearly the remarkable transition which had occurred in architectural form over 30 years.

What also stands out in Svacha's account, as Kenneth Frampton points out in his Foreword, is the remarkable interaction between all the arts of the period – visual and literary. The forum for Kotera's new architecture was the literary and artistic Manes Artists' Association; Janak's Cubism grew out of the Group of Visual Artists' 'New Primitivism'; while the Emotional Functionalism of the 30s returned to Manes. Nowhere is this interaction more clearly exemplified than in the Cubist style with its transposition of the startling visual language of Picasso

and Braque into the multifaceted surfaces and broken space of buildings such as Gocar's Black Madonna Department Store and Chochol's Modek Apartment Building. Flicking through the biographies at the end of the book confirms Frampton's view that 'there was perhaps no other 20th-century avant-garde that so readily transgressed the boundaries between the different arts'.

Linked to this is the Czech critical awareness and assimilation of contemporary international trends in architecture. The modern style had its roots in the *Wagnerschule*; for its affluent suburbs it looked to the example of Unwin's Garden City Movement and the vernacular revival in England; and Le Corbusier's work, frequently published in the proliferation of journals and reviews which marked the period, exerted a huge influence on the suburban villa form and Purism; while the Functionalists looked to Constructivist developments in the Soviet Union.

What emerges from Svacha's detailed exposition of the many and varied movements in Czech architecture between the *Manifesto of the Czech Modern* and the outbreak of World War II (or, to all intents and purposes, Hitler's annexation of Czechoslovakia in 1939) is the varied and fiercely fought interpretation as to what architecture should be and what it should do. While the formal purity of some of the Functionalist buildings illustrated cannot be denied, its complete abrogation of artistic and psychological values must be questioned; as must Cubism's rejection of social need and rationalism in pursuit of a pure aesthetic. Svacha's implicit conclusion is that architecture 'does not proceed mechanically from purpose to its formal expression, but pulsates between the two, oscillates between the technical possibilities and the individuality of the artist's creative energy'. Hence he looks with trepidation at the current revival of Functionalist forms removed from their former left-wing, avant-garde substance. *R Bean*

BEYOND THE REVOLUTION

THEATRE SPIRAL, PRAGUE, BY TOMAS KULIK, JAN LOUDA,
JINDRICH SMETANA AND ZBYSEK STYBLO

Architectural Design

BEYOND THE REVOLUTION
THE ARCHITECTURE OF EASTERN EUROPE

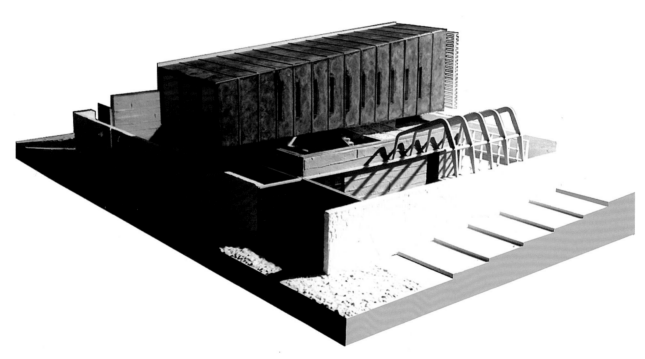

EXIT HOUSE, EXIT; OPPOSITE: RECONSTRUCTION AND COURTYARD EXTENSION OF THE CZECH CHAMBER OF LAWYERS,
PRAGUE, KRUPAUER, STRITECKY AND ATELIER 8000

ACADEMY EDITIONS · LONDON

Acknowledgements

We would like to thank all of our contributors for their enthusiasm and assistance in preparing this issue; in particular to Ron Kenley for his help in establishing contacts in Eastern Europe. On behalf of Ron Witte, we would also like to thank Sarah Whiting, Juliet Koss, Professor Russell Berman at Stanford University and the National Endowment for the Humanities for their assistance. The illustrations to Ron Witte's essay 'Berlin by Night' and 'Stadtschloss' are reproduced from *Unvergessenes Berlin*, 1968 and Palast der Republik is from the competition booklet *Internationaler Städtbaulicher Ideenwettbewerb*. The illustrations to Ron Kenley's essay 'Arc' are video stills taken from the film *Architecture and Power*, written by Augustin Ioan, directed by Nicolae Margineanu and produced by Agerfilm and the Union of Romanian Architects, 1992. Takuro Hoshino, Peter Hasdell, Alain Chiaradia, Neave Brown, Robert Mull, Ilva Kist, Joost Grootens, Khalid Mehmood, Filipe Decorte all collaborated with Raoul Bunschoten for CHORA Institute for Architecture and Urbanism. We also thank, on behalf of CHORA, Vyacheslav Glazychev, Elena Kolpinsky and Vladimir Lalyakin of the AEU. Ivan Straus' diary excerpt 'Architecture and Barbarians' was translated and edited by Aleksandra Wagner from the original manuscript of Ivan Straus' diaries.

Front and Inside Covers: Lebbeus Woods, Bosnia Free-State, The Wall

Photographic Credits

All material is courtesy of the authors and architects unless otherwise stated.
Attempts have been made to locate sources of all photographs to obtain full reproduction rights, but in the very few cases where this process has failed to find the copyright holder, apologies are offered.
Steve Ibbotsen *p29 above;* Ester Havlova *p46;* Ales Jungmann *p36;* OKO *pp54, 56, 57, 58, 59;* Ioana Vasile and Raluca Visinescu *p29 centre, below;* Mark Salette *p44;* Ivan Straus *p65;* Slapal Stach *p2;* Pavel Stecha *pp1, 38, 44, 52, 53;* Michal Tuma *p6;* Zeljko Puljic *p64*

EDITOR: Maggie Toy
EDITORIAL TEAM: Iona Baird, Stephen Watt, Cristina Fontoura
ART EDITOR: Andrea Bettella CHIEF DESIGNER: Mario Bettella DESIGNER: Steven Roberts

CONSULTANTS: Catherine Cooke, Terry Farrell, Kenneth Frampton, Charles Jencks, Heinrich Klotz, Leon Krier, Robert Maxwell, Demetri Porphyrios, Kenneth Powell, Colin Rowe, Derek Walker

First published in Great Britain in 1996 by *Architectural Design* an imprint of
ACADEMY GROUP LTD, 42 LEINSTER GARDENS, LONDON W2 3AN
Member of the VCH Publishing Group
ISBN: 1 8540 254 7 (UK)

Distributed to the trade in the United States of America by
NATIONAL BOOK NETWORK INC, 4720 BOSTON WAY, LANHAM, MARYLAND, 20706

Printed and bound in Italy

Contents

NERATOV, PRESERVATION OF A RUINED CHURCH, EAST BOHEMIA, SIAL, 1994

ARCHITECTURAL DESIGN PROFILE No 119

BEYOND THE REVOLUTION

EDITORIAL
Maggie Toy

In the turmoil which follows a revolution shock waves are felt on all levels; socially, culturally and demographically. Inevitably there is an impact on architecture and urban design. This effect can perhaps only be detected a short while after the revolution, as the development starts and the changes begin to show. The architectural language of the former Communist regimes is an emotive one, of bitterness and division: walls, barriers, wounds, oppression, totalitarianism. In the six or seven years since the revolutions of Eastern Europe it would be ideal if we could say that the evolving language has become more optimistic and less troubled. Certainly, the removal of the Berlin Wall has led to the rapidly burgeoning economy of a unified Germany and Prague, and the Czech Republic in particular have certainly achieved unprecedented levels of development. All of these changes affect the spirit of the people and of the city. Is this having a positive effect on the urban environment and are people calling for an improved state of architecture? Is there an attempt to replicate what is seen elsewhere in Western societies or is the new found freedom permitting a new style of design which combines the lessons of old with the excitement of the new?

Evidently, the transition has not been easy or as straightforward everywhere and in the states of Bosnia-Herzegovina, Croatia and Serbia, conflict still rages over the definition of boundaries and ethnic origins. The diary of Ivan Straus emotively describes the vast devastation, and only serves to reinforce the importance of political and ideological structures. The difficulties of creating a positive urban environment have been faced by Lebbeus Woods and his projects presented here graphically illustrate his intimacy with the problems and his finesse in contributing to their heuristic resolution.

There is a prevalent spirit of hope and destiny, a new architectural destiny. While architecture cannot be said to have informed the revolutionary changes, architects have played a prominent role. In the Ion Mincu Institute of Architecture in Bucharest the students were at the front-line of the struggles to obtain freedom from the dictator Ceausescu. The Romanian recovery is described by Ioana-Maria Sandi as having an incredible potential for development but one which must learn from previous mistakes and ensure that progress is made slowly in order not to fall victim to the regimes of capitalism or of blanket appropriation of Western values.

In the Czech Republic, by comparison, the centre of Prague has already become developed by foreign investors and tourist industries and the authorities are having to implement remedial action, in terms of planning restrictions, to limit the extent of the change in order that damage to the existing social and urban structures is minimal.

Frank Gehry's intervention in the city centre, which has created great interest, demonstrates his ability to generate stunning architectural forms within the city context, while Roman Koucky's publishing house provides an interesting and exquisitely detailed reconstruction within an existing building.

The executors of the projects presented demonstrate an accomplished level of competency in dealing with these challenges. It is worth considering what we can take from such experience and instead of assuming that the learning is a one-way process, begin to absorb some of the determination and tolerance portrayed by these architects.

Work by Atelier Loegler & Partners in Poland clearly demonstrates the freedom of design and optimism currently reflected in society.

The European Community is paying close attention to the activities in the countries which impinge on its periphery: Croatia has already applied for membership. This political motivation has implications on the architecture and urban environment. Chora, a newly formed organisation, is currently working with local authorities in both Alexandrov near Moscow and Zagreb, Croatia to develop urban planning strategies for areas which, since the revolution, have dramatically changed and therefore need completely reassessing.

It is important that social and political experience informs architecture and the built environment. It is vital that these Eastern European countries, freed from oppression by the insurgent events of the recent past, maintain their pride in their own history and develop accordingly, manufacturing a slow steady growth on their own terms.

Commercial bank in Ceske Budejovice, Martin Krupauer, Jiri Stritecky and Atelier 8000

7

NEIL LEACH
ARCHITECTURE OR REVOLUTION?

'*Architecture ou Révolution . . . It is the question of building which lies at the root of the social unrest of today; architecture or revolution.*'[1] Le Corbusier, 1922.

Le Corbusier, in common with many architects of the Modern Movement, was convinced of the social role of architecture. In an era of great social and political change, he perceived architecture as a crucial instrument in addressing the ills of contemporary society. An appropriate architecture would combat social unrest. Le Corbusier viewed architecture as a means to avoid revolution, while the architects of post-revolutionary Russia saw architecture as a way of supporting the aims and ideals of a Marxist revolution. Architectural theorists, such as Alexei Gan and Moisei Ginzburg, looked to architecture to resolve the particular problems of post-revolutionary Marxist society. Buildings should not simply reflect passively changing social conditions; they should be active instruments of change. For Gan and Ginzburg buildings themselves were 'revolutionary',[2] and were to operate as active social condensers.

Le Corbusier's position seems diametrically opposed to that of Gan and Ginzburg. Yet an alternative reading is possible, and it could be argued that Le Corbusier spoke of avoiding political 'revolution' not because he was opposed to the concept of revolution, but rather because he recognised in architecture the possibility of a 'revolution' that would go beyond the political. As Fredric Jameson has observed, 'he saw the construction and the constitution of new spaces as the most revolutionary act, and one that could "replace" the narrowly political revolution of the mere seizure of power.'[3] Thus, far from being against revolution, Le Corbusier could be seen as a supporter of reform in its most radical and far-reaching sense. It is clear that both Le Corbusier and the architects of the new Russia recognised in architecture the same potential, the possibility of alleviating social problems and of creating a new and better world. Architecture for the pioneers of the Modern Movement had a role as a democratic force within a democratic society. Architecture was to be a force of liberation, overtly political and emancipatory in its outlook.

At the other end of the 20th century, in the light of the recent 'revolutions' in Central and Eastern Europe the relationship between architecture and revolution deserves further consideration. Clearly, it needs to be interrogated beyond the naive utopianism of the Modern Movement. The term 'revolution' should not be taken lightly, nor treated uncritically. It may be too easily appropriated to dress up shifts in political power, which, far from overturning a previous regime, merely replicate the *status quo* in an alternative formal variant. Too easily, also, such a term may be smuggled into empty slogans and adopted by the artistic avant-garde to refer to merely ephemeral changes in fashion.

Architecture and revolution: these terms need to reconsidered and their relationship rethought. Can architecture claim to have an influence on the social or political realm and what is its status as a force of social change? What links aesthetics and politics? What relationship may there be between architecture and revolution? Can there indeed be a 'revolutionary' architecture?

Aesthetics and revolution

The argument for a link between aesthetics and revolution has been made most forcefully by Herbert Marcuse. For Marcuse the revolutionary may exist within the aesthetic. Although he addresses literature, the same situation, he claims, would apply to all forms of art including architecture.[4] Marcuse goes beyond traditional Marxist aesthetics which views art as an expression of social relations, to perceive art as a potential critique of social relations. It is precisely the aesthetic form of art which allows this: 'In its autonomy', Marcuse claims, 'art both protests these relations, and at the same time transcends them. Art therefore subverts the dominant consciousness, the ordinary experience'.[5] From this he concludes that art can be revolutionary in the stylistic changes that it brings about, which disrupt accepted aesthetic conventions and reflect broader social changes. But beyond the domain of the technical, art can also be revolutionary in a more direct fashion. Art can represent the 'prevailing unfreedom', and can therefore break through 'the mystified (and petrified) social reality'. Thus art can be liberational by opening up 'the horizon of change'. 'In this sense, every authentic work of art would be revolutionary, ie subversive of perception and understanding, an indictment of the established reality, the appearance of the image of liberation.'[6]

For Marcuse, art was necessarily abstracted from the given social reality by a process of sublimation. The material was thereby reshaped according to the rules of aesthetic form. Art therefore came both to represent reality and to challenge it, by shattering the 'reified objectivity of established social relations'.[7] Art was for Marcuse a reinterpretation of reality transported to the realm of the aesthetic. Art can function, in its aesthetic form, as a critical force in the struggle for liberation, not through some empty notion of pure form, but by virtue of its content having become form.

Marcuse is quite categorical, then, in his support for a revolutionary aesthetic. Yet his position amounts to a deeply utopian one, and can be challenged on several accounts. In contrast to mainstream Marxist aesthetics, art for Marcuse was not proletarian. He remained deeply suspicious of the mass media which he would see as the 'principal agent of an engineered social consensus that denied real human interests'.[8] In common with Theodor Adorno he could be accused of promoting an elitist notion of art – a 'high' art. Adorno himself presents a more recondite elaboration of the role of art, and draws a distinction between the unifying and pacifying nature of the 'culture industry' and art proper. Post-Modern thinkers would argue that Adorno's treatment of the 'culture industry' is overly simplistic and monolithic, and that it does not allow for resistance within popular culture itself.[9] This criticism of Adorno could equally be levelled at Marcuse, whose celebration of an autonomous art fails to recognise the critical capacity of more popular forms of cultural expression.

Marcuse's position is also questionable on other accounts. Even accepting a view of art as autonomous, it could be argued that any attempt to politicise art must be compromised in its very nature. It is as though an effective opposition can be detected between politics and art. Walter Benjamin exposed the problem in his essay, 'The Work of Art in the Age of Mechanical Reproduction'.[10] Benjamin explored the problem of how Fascism used aesthetics to celebrate war. The aestheticisation of war by the Futurists, in particular, succeeded in masking the immorality of war, by transporting it into the realm of aesthetics. In effect it could be extrapolated from Benjamin's argument that aesthetics brings about an anaesthetisation of the political, and this applied not only to Fascism but to any form of politics.[11] Yet, almost paradoxically, Benjamin concludes the article with the comment, 'This is the situation in politics which Fascism is rendering aesthetic. Communism responds by politicising art.'[12] There is, as Susan Buck-Morss has observed, an inherent contradiction in this last comment. In order for aesthetics to become politicised, as Buck-Morss notes, the term 'would shift its meaning 180 degrees. "Aesthetics" would be transformed, indeed, redeemed, so that, ironically (or dialectically), it would describe the field in which the antidote to Fascism is deployed as a political response.'[13] If aesthetics has the effect of anaesthetising politics, the possibility of a politicised aesthetic must therefore be compromised, since whatever political content is associated with art will itself be anaesthetised by that art.

Beyond this, there are further problems over the question of political content in a work of art. Where art is not being used in a directly communicative manner – as slogans or advertising – the nature of its engagement with its audience is mediated by the very abstraction of its aesthetic form, and its capacity to communicate 'political content' is therefore compromised. Nor should it be assumed that the reception of that content on the part of the reader is unproblematic, unless one is to resort to a hermeneutics of reading. Yet the shortcomings of hermeneutics – and indeed the whole project of phenomenology – have been all too often exposed. In effect, the reading of any work of art is problematic, and although there have been attempts by Habermas and others to overcome 'death of the author' arguments by introducing a notion of intersubjective communication, the bare fact remains that there can be no single privileged reading of a work of art.

Within the context of the whole aesthetics and politics debate, the relationship between an ideology of the aesthetic and a more general ideology needs to be considered. What underpinned much Modernist art was the attempt to challenge existing conventions. In this sense Modernist art was 'revolutionary'. Yet there is a danger in conflating the aesthetic with the social. An aesthetic 'revolution' which challenges the values and norms of the world of art should be distinguished from a social revolution which challenges the existing power structures within a broader political context. The confusion which seems to have beset much Modernist art in its claims to be 'revolutionary' beyond the realm of the aesthetic has been to equate the aesthetic with the social. In effect there has been an elision – a sleight of hand – which attempts to legitimate a connection which ought to be seen as no more than allegorical. Yet this is not to deny that the two realms, of aesthetic and social, may intersect on occasion, so that the aesthetic revolution may engage directly with the social revolution under a specific constellation of circumstances. The possibility of such an event is perhaps greater in the context of architecture, where the involvement with the social is more direct than in other forms of aesthetic expression.

Ideology and architecture

Architecture poses a special question. Architecture is deeply embedded within economic and other structures of power, and its capacity to operate as a critical force of change is therefore compromised. The architect, furthermore, is no free agent, and can act only vicariously on behalf of the client. If any authorial position is sought, therefore, we should perhaps look to the client rather than to the architect. Architecture also has its own special significance as the most public of all the arts, and the one which may most acutely influence the social. This distinguishes architecture from other arts, in that its capacity to act autonomously – in Marcuse's terms – as a critical commentary on the realm of the real, is compromised by its instantiation within that realm. The very presence of architecture gives it a social impact, so that any 'negativity', any critical capacity within architecture, is all but cancelled by the 'positivity' of its presence. The very physicality of architecture always threatens to install a new status quo, and undermines its capacity to be 'subversive'.

Yet the problem of a revolutionary architecture has to be addressed ultimately within the context of the more general question of architecture and its influence on the social realm. Within the popular imagination there has been little doubt about architecture's capacity to condition a response within the user. Indeed the common view seems to be encapsulated in Georges Bataille's 'definition' of architecture. For him (monumental) architecture not only reflects the politics of an epoch, but also has a marked influence on the social.

Architecture is the expression of the true nature of society, as physiognomy is the expression of the nature of the individuals. However, this comparison is applicable, above all, to the physiognomy of officials (prelates, magistrates, admirals). In fact, only society's ideal nature – that of authoritative command and prohibition – expresses itself in actual architectural constructions. Thus great monuments rise up like dams, opposing a logic of majesty and authority on all unquiet elements; it is in the form of cathedrals and palaces that the church and state speak to and impose silence upon the crowds.[14]

Such a view, however, must not go unchallenged. The interaction between architecture and the political deserves to be interrogated further. This is not to deny, of course, the status of architecture as a political act. Certainly, if we are to believe Stanley Fish, every act, including the architectural, is inscribed within some ideological position.[15] There is no platform, Fish states, which is not constrained by some ideological imperative. Indeed there needs to be an ideological content in that this is precisely what gives an act its force. This may not be obvious because ideology remains largely invisible, yet it is through its very invisibility that ideology derives its potential. Ideology constitutes a form of background level of consciousness which influences all our actions.

A distinction must be made, however, between the act of building itself and subsequent semantic 'readings' of that building. The political content of the act of building is perhaps the more obvious, but it is more often overlooked and forgotten. In the case of the Stalinallee in Berlin, for example, the act of building was deeply political and was marked by considerable social unrest. Demonstrations erupted on 16 June 1953 against the low level of pay for building workers, and spread the following day to other parts of the city.[16] As could be expected these protests were brutally suppressed, and about a dozen demonstrators were killed. Yet what dominates discussion of the Stalinallee is not this all but forgotten moment in its construction, but the question of whether the project can be read semantically as 'totalitarian'.[17]

It is precisely in the these semantic readings of architecture that the fragility of associations between architecture and politics becomes most apparent. In their discussion of 'democratic' architecture, Charles Jencks and Maggie Valentine recognise the subject as problematic. They observe that neither Frank Lloyd Wright nor Vincent Scully, managed to relate politics to any typology or style of building.[18] Yet while they also note that Aldo Rossi and others had claimed that there was no direct link between style and ideology, they themselves persist in an attempt to define an 'architecture of democracy'. Their approach relies on semantic readings. For Jencks and Valentine, as it transpires, the problem rests ultimately in the complex 'codes' which 'democratic architecture' adopts. It must avoid excessive uniformity ('An architecture of democracy that is uniform is as absurd as a democracy of identical citizens') yet equally it should avoid excessive variety ('an architecture where every building is in a different style is as privatised as a megalopolis of consumers.') 'Thus a democratic style . . . is at once shared, abstract, individualised and disharmonious.'[19] Jencks and Valentine emphasise the aesthetic dimension, as though this has some direct bearing on the political. Yet their argument is undone by its own internal inconsistencies. How can classical architecture symbolise both Greek democracy and Italian fascism? Can there ever be any essential politics to a style of architecture or even exist a 'democratic architecture'? We may recognise the naivety of the Jeffersonian 'grid-iron' plan, carpeted across the USA in an effort to promote democracy.

Manfredo Tafuri, on the other hand, rejects outright a semantic approach to architecture. Such an approach is ultimately tautological, and succeeds only in describing the architectural work, and never in *explaining* it.[20] Moreover, this approach risks conflating the political with the aesthetic. While Tafuri's writing is frequently difficult and often obscure, his outlook rests on certain clear beliefs. In particular, Tafuri is unequivocal in his separation of the aesthetic from the political. As Fredric Jameson observes:

> The architectural critic [for Tafuri] has no business being an 'ideologist', that is, a visionary proponent of architectural styles of the future, 'revolutionary' architecture and the like: her role must be resolutely negative, the vigilant denunciation of existent or historical ideologies.[21]

Tafuri himself comments, 'Today, indeed the principal task of ideological criticism is to do away with impotent and ineffectual myths, which so often serve as illusions that permit the survival of anachronistic "hopes in design".'[22]

Therefore for Tafuri architects cannot hope to achieve a 'revolutionary' or utopian architecture. Architecture cannot be political – indeed there is a complete break between aesthetics and politics – although architects themselves may act politically as individuals. Tafuri, then, emphasises a politics of practice, and challenges the notion of a politics of the aesthetic. Yet, while there can be no 'revolutionary' architecture, architecture can none the less provide the forum for a 'revolutionary' political *praxis*. Tafuri therefore opens the way for a 'politics of space.' Indeed Fredric Jameson concludes his review of Tafuri's writings with the comment that there may be something to be said after all for a Lefebvrean 'politics of space'.[23]

There is often a radical disjuncture between semantic readings of a building and the politics of use of that building. As Adrian Rifkin has pointed out in the context of Jean Nouvel's building in Paris, *L'Institute du Monde Arabe*, one might discover more about the 'ideology' of that building not by reading the 'arabesque' semantic coding of its facade – which in Rifkin's eyes is decidedly kitsch – but by observing the politics of use of the building.[24] While the Institute restaurants and galleries are patronised largely by Europeans, they are serviced largely by Arabs. Although Nouvel might have intended the building to celebrate Arab culture, the politics of its use indicate that it merely replicates the same cultural imperialism which is at play elsewhere in Paris.

The use of space can therefore be political, even if the aesthetic cannot be. Yet one might still argue that architecture – in its very physical form – must indeed be political, through the influence that it exerts on the users of a building. In other words there is an association to be made between the form of a space and the political *praxis* within that space. This prompts the further question as to whether architecture in its physical form may somehow influence the politics of use.

Space, knowledge and power

One of the central preoccupations for Michel Foucault is the relationship between power and space, and he throws some light on this issue in his discussion of Bentham's panopticon. In this piece, Foucault explores the question of how architectural form may influence social behaviour. The plan for a prison, the panopticon has a central tower surrounded by cells arranged radially. The guard sits in the tower, and is afforded a view into each of the cells. Meanwhile, the openings in the tower itself, through blinds and other devices, prevent the inmates in the cells from knowing whether or not the guard is looking at them. Thus the inmates remain under the perpetually controlling gaze of the guard.[25] The principle which Foucault is trying to illustrate is that the architecture may become an apparatus for 'for creating and sustaining a power relationship independent of the person who operates it.'[26] In other words it is the architectural form of the panopticon which helps to engender a form of social control. Such an example would seem to suggest the possibility of architecture determining social behaviour.

In a subsequent interview with Paul Rabinow, Foucault acknowledges that architects are not necessarily 'the masters of space' that they once were, or believed themselves to be.[27] Thus he appears to qualify this position on the capacity for architecture to determine social behaviour. On the question of whether there could be an architecture which would act as a force of either liberation or oppression, Foucault concludes that 'liberation' and 'oppression' are not mutually exclusive, and that even in that most oppressive of structures, some form of 'resistance' may be in operation. Liberty, for Foucault, is a practice, that cannot be 'established by the project itself'. 'The liberty of men is never assured by the institutions and laws that are intended to guarantee them.'[28]

Architecture therefore cannot in itself be liberative or repressive. As Foucault comments, 'I think that it can never be inherent in the structure of things to guarantee the exercise of freedom. The guarantee of freedom is freedom.'[29] Architectural form, he concludes, cannot in itself resolve social problems. Only politics can address them, although architecture can contribute in some way, provided it is in league with the political. Thus Foucault concludes: 'I think that [architecture] can and does produce positive effects when the liberating intentions of the architect coincide with the real practice of people in the exercise of their freedom.'[30] Foucault is therefore not contradicting but merely qualifying his earlier comments on the panopticon. It is not the form of the panopticon which controls the behaviour of the inmates. Rather it is the politics of use – the fact that the building is operating as a prison – which is ultimately determinant of behaviour, and the architecture is merely supporting the politics of use through its efficient layout.

10

The Foucault's position on this is clear. In opposition to the utopian visions of Marcuse and others, Foucault would emphasise the politics of everyday life over architectural form as the principle determinant of social behaviour. 'The architect', he comments, 'has no power over me.'[31] According to such an approach, there could be no 'revolutionary' architecture in the Marcusian sense of an architecture that might constitute some critical force of change. Yet this is not to deny the capacity for architecture to 'produce positive effects' when it is in league with the practice of politics. Certainly, this introduces an important temporal dimension into consideration. As political practice changes, so the efficacy of the architectural form to support that practice may itself be compromised.

After the revolution

Architecture is traditionally seen as built ideology, yet the problem is considerably more complex than might first appear. Buildings, according to the logic of Foucault's argument would have no inherent politics, if by 'politics' we infer a capacity to influence the social. Rather a building may facilitate – to a greater or lesser extent – the practice of those politics through its very physical form. The supposed democracy of an anti-hierarchical, uniform layout such as the grid, was of course challenged by the use of that form in the layout of that most anti-democratic of spaces, the concentration camp.

It is a question rather of what political associations a building may have. What is in operation in any attribution of politics to architecture is a form of 'mapping', whereby a building is endowed with ideological content according to a certain configuration of *praxis*. As that *praxis* shifts, so too does the 'content' of that building. Thus the pyramids, emblems of tyranny and oppression to the slaves who constructed them, take on different associations in the age of tourism.

According to Fredric Jameson what is important is the question of history. Associations rely on the collective memory. A building must be viewed within a transhistorical context. Without any sense of history a building will lose its ideological associations. Towards the end of Nicolae Ceausescu's dictatorship of Romania and immediately after his execution, his Palace in Bucharest was universally decried. It was denounced as totalitarian architecture, as a symbol of Ceausescu's regime, and compared to the architecture of other such regimes. After the revolution, it would appear that the population was in favour of destroying this monument to dictatorship. Some years later most architects continue to deride the building, while attitudes of the majority of the population would seem to be in favour of it: the building has emerged as a popular conference venue, and the monumental avenue leading up to the palace is now the most expensive real estate in Bucharest. For many the palace represents the centre of the city.[32]

What then is the ideological status of this building? One could argue that only the construction of the building – which itself entailed the destruction of some precious remnants of old Bucharest – could be construed as ideological. Any subsequent reading of the constructed edifice, however, must be based on aesthetic and not political criteria, even though the aesthetic terminology of 'reactionary' or 'totalitarian' may ape the political. The building itself may only be *associated* with an ideological position, but that association relies on the collective memory of the people. As that memory fades, so the building may be re-appropriated according to new ideological imperatives: shifting its symbolic content from monument to Communist dictatorship to temple of high capitalism, in a mechanism not dissimilar to the 'floating signs' of the fashion system. Therefore we may conclude that if we are looking for a link between architecture and revolution, such a link may exist only in the realm of shifting semantic associations.

Notes

1 Corbusier, *Towards a New Architecture*, trans F Etchells, Butterworth Architecture, (London), 1989, p269. *Architecture ou Révolution* was the original title of *Vers Une Architecture*.
2 See Catherine Cooke, *Russian Avant-Garde: Theories of Art, Architecture and the City*, Academy Editions, (London), 1995, p118.
3 Fredric Jameson, 'Architecture and the Critique of Ideology', ed Joan Ockman, *Architecture, Criticism, Ideology*, Princeton Architectural Press, (Princeton), 1985, p71.
4 Herbert Marcuse, *The Aesthetic Dimension: Towards a Critique of Marxist Aesthetics*, Macmillan Press, (London), 1978, px.
5 Ibid, pix.
6 Ibid, pxi.
7 Ibid, p7.
8 For Marcuse on mass culture see C A Rootes, "Mass Culture" in eds William Outhwaite and Tom Bottomore, *The Blackwell Dictionary of Twentieth-Century Social Thought*, Blackwell, (London), 1993, pp369-370.
9 See the comments of J Bernstein , 'Theodor Adorno', *The Culture Industry*, ed J Bernstein, Routledge, (London), 1991.
10 Walter Benjamin, 'The Work of Art in the Age of Mechanical Reproduction', *Illuminations*, trans Harry Zohn, Fontana Press, (London), 1973, pp211-235.
11 The link between aesthetics and anaesthetics has been explored by Susan Buck-Morss, 'Aesthetics and Anaesthetics: Walter Benjamin's Artwork Essay Reconsidered', *October*, 62, Fall 1992, pp3-41.
12 Walter Benjamin, op cit, p235.
13 Susan Buck-Morss, op cit, p5.
14 Georges Bataille, 'Architecture', trans D Faccini, *October*, 60, Spring 1992, pp25-6.
15 Stanley Fish, *There's No Such Thing as Free Speech – And It's a Good Thing Too*, Oxford University Press, (Oxford), 1994.
16 Bernard Newman, *Behind the Berlin Wall*, Robert Hale, (London), 1964, pp31-42.
17 Tafuri, in contrast to other commentators, reads the project not from a political perspective, but strictly in terms of urban planning 'aesthetic' objectives. Manfredo Tafuri and Francesco Dal Co, *Modern Architecture*, Abrams, (New York), 1979, pp322, 326.
18 Charles Jencks and Maggie Valentine, 'The Architecture of Democracy: The Hidden Tradition', *Architectural Design*, Profile 69, Academy Editions, (London), 1987, pp8-25. For Vincent Scully on architecture and democracy see Vincent Scully, *Modern Architecture: The Architecture of Democracy*, George Braziller, (New York), 1974; for Frank Lloyd Wright on the subject see: Frank Lloyd Wright, 'An Organic Architecture', *The Architecture of Democracy*, Lund Humphries, (London), 1939; *When Democracy Builds*, University of Chicago Press, (Chicago), 1945.
19 Ibid, p25.
20 Manfredo Tafuri, *Architecture and Utopia*, trans B Luigi La Penta, MIT Press, (Cambridge, Mass), 1976, p165. See also Tafuri, *Theories and History of Architecture*, Granada, (London), 1980, pp176ff.
21 Fredric Jameson, op cit, p53.
22 Manfredo Tafuri, *Architecture and Utopia*, op cit, p182.
23 Fredric Jameson, op cit, p87.
24 Adrian Rifkin, in lecture delivered to students on the MA in Architecture and Critical Theory course, University of Nottingham, May, 1995.
25 Although Bentham's panopticon was never built, the principle can be seen in numerous buildings, such as James Stirling's Seeley History Library, Cambridge. Here the control desk is positioned centrally, all the desks and shelves laid out radially around it, allowing the librarian to monitor the entire space. A sophisticated form of panopticism is closed circuit surveillance cameras.
26 *Discipline and Punish*, trans Alan Sheridan, Penguin, (London), 1979, p201.
27 Paul Rabinow (ed), *The Foucault Reader*, Penguin, (London), 1991, p244.
28 Ibid, p245.
29 Ibid.
30 Ibid, p246.
31 Ibid, p247.
32 The popularity of the building among the general public was endorsed when in July 1995, George Hagi, the international footballer and public icon in Romania, held his wedding reception there.

FROM ABOVE: Berlin at night; the Palast der Republik; the Stadschloss

RON WITTE

NEW WHIRLED ORDER

BERLIN

Those who stood among the ruins of the Wall and pronounced a 'New World Order' were misled. The major changes provoked, either directly or indirectly, by the groundswell of 1989 – German unification, the Gulf War, the explosion of the USSR, conflicts in the ex-Yugoslavia, the UN crisis – prevent us from recognising even a mediocre new order. In fact, the world has become more dangerous, more complicated, its uncertainties multiplied, its anguishes and fears of all kinds intensified.[1]

With the collapse of the Wall, Berlin became the locus of New Worldism. Newness was everywhere: Berlin was poised to be the economic centre of a new Europe that in turn was entering a new global solidarity. In 1989 the city began to situate itself within a suddenly dominant socio-economic climate combining George Bush's New World Order with the aspirations of a nascent European Union. This ideological fusion engendered a rhetoric of newness that was at the very least premature and at the very worst a mask dangerously concealing pressures within an allegedly now-perfect sphere of international relations. Blinded at times by such excessively luminous New Worldism, Berlin's planners began to 'lay foundations for the new, stable development in the heart of [the] city'.[2] Their quest for stability was an obvious response to the city's recent division; it also invoked New Worldism's idealising tendencies, tendencies which smoothed over those socio-economic issues within the city that did not conform to New Worldism's tenets. In Germany, many of these non-conforming issues descended from GDR social policies: abortion rights, childcare programmes, housing regulations and labour laws. Various aspects of these GDR policies were incompatible with West German social structures and were consequently realigned so as to stabilise the reunified social contract.

The editing of GDR social policies has paralleled the methodical elimination of many of the symbolic urban traces of the GDR. Changes to one of Berlin's most important public areas, Marx-Engels Platz, exemplify the extent to which Berlin's urban spaces have been reconsidered and reconstructed so as to create a unified urban trajectory, whose cohesiveness depends on a stable historical framework. While the history chosen to develop this framework, that of Karl Friedrich Schinkel, is undoubtedly significant, many of the individuals engaged in Berlin's current planning process depend on Schinkel's legacy to substantiate their commitment to an overzealous stability-envy. These planners and civic leaders often ignore the fact that the city sits at the head of not *one* but *several* histories.

Shattered Engagements

Berlin's preoccupation with its own turbulent history is not new. Prior to World War II, and before the Iron Curtain created a caricature of the city's heterogeneity, Siegfried Kracauer explored a provocative alternative to Berlin's ongoing struggle to overcome instability. In his writings for the *Frankfurter Zeitung* from 1920 until his dismissal in 1933, Kracauer wavered between a fascination with 'the experience of [Berlin] as a labyrinth of fragmentary signs'[3] and a panicked horror of its indecipherability. Rather than envying the *grandes histoires* of Europe's great capitals – histories that gave Paris, Vienna, and London cohesive characters – Kracauer looked for Berlin's identity within its historical detachment:

> . . . only in Berlin are the transformations of the past so radically stripped from memory. Many experience precisely this life from headline to headline as exciting; partly because they profit from the fact that their earlier existence vanishes in its moment of disappearing, partly because they believe they are living twice as much when they are living in the present.[4]

It was not without trepidation that Kracauer looked out at the city. The lights of Berlin, emanating from neon signs and falling upon the monuments of the city, illuminated labour's search for distraction. Berlin's glowing evenings were a kind of edge, a night-time periphery into which workers could pass in order to leave behind the 'tension which fill[ed] their day fully, without making it filling'.[5] At the same time, Kracauer recognised that this City Without History shimmered with a potential future. Berlin's numerous neon signs 'shot beyond the economy . . . what [was] intended as advertisement [was] transformed into illumination'. For Kracauer, the luminosity of this electric aura elevated the 'cult of distraction' to the level of a culture 'aimed at the masses'. Unlike the post-1989 advocates of historical stability, Kracauer was unable, and unwilling, to fabricate a past; instead he found a neon halo *within* Berlin's present artifice. The modern metropolis hurled itself against the lens through which he peered, shattering the glass without destroying the lens, and revealing Berlin's true face: a glittering, atomised urbanity in which past and present coalesced in the glass' ever changing two-dimensional surface.

In 1932, Kracauer wrote that Berlin:

> . . . has the magical means of eradicating all memories. It is present-day and, moreover, it makes a point of honour of being absolutely present-day. Whoever stays for any length of time in Berlin hardly knows in the end where he actually came from. His existence is not like a line but a series of points . . .[6]

These points are the shards of a fractured urban tradition whose ahistorical ground is blamed for Berlin's disfigured state. On the other hand, when these points are seen through the kaleidoscopic lens of Kracauer's eye, their entropic framing of Berlin's urban space allows the city to inhale the multifarious air of modernity. Between these points can be found the city's emergent possibilities. Kracauer distinguishes the differences:

> . . . between two types of images of the city . . . those that are consciously formed and others that reveal themselves unintentionally. The former have their origin in the artificial intention that is realised in squares, vistas, groups of buildings and perspectival effects that Baedeker illuminates with a small star. In contrast, the latter emerge without having been previously

planned. They are not compositions . . . but rather fortuitous creations that do not allow themselves to be called to account.[7] The unintentional, the fortuitous, the emergent. Kracauer's is a language of impermanence, of a fleeting present. But it is also a language of potential, of provocation, of engagement. These terms describe a non-conclusive metropolitan space whose figure is simultaneously legible and amoebic. The difference between Baedeker's stars – guidebook notations for significant monuments – and Kracauer's points is that of an urban space which *prescribes permanent* occupation versus an urban space which *catalyses temporal* occupation.

As a means of understanding the built public realm, these two categorisations – permanency and temporality – can be developed from Nancy Fraser's reading of Jürgen Habermas' singular definition of the public sphere. Fraser critiques the singularity of Habermas' model, questioning his assertion that 'the emergence of additional publics are symptomatic . . . of fragmentation and decline' in the public sphere. The attempt to define a unique public sphere, she argues, requires its participants to consent to its terms. Such obligatory consent constitutes a 'hegemonic mode of domination' in that it eliminates all non-dominant voices:

> . . . public life in egalitarian, multi-cultural societies cannot consist exclusively in a single, comprehensive public sphere. That would be tantamount to filtering diverse rhetorical and stylistic norms through a single, overarching lens. Moreover, since there is no such lens that is genuinely culturally neutral, it would effectively privilege the expressive norms of one cultural group over others, thereby making discursive assimilation a condition for participation in public debate.[8]

In a manner that is similar to Kracauer's kaleidoscopic view of the city, Fraser sees multiple publics, or dissenting voices, as not only non-threatening but *requisite* to the survival of a non-exclusive public sphere. The Baedeker stars to which Kracauer refers are concrete markers for the 'must see' points in the city; they reinforce a particular history and, through their assertion of lineage, signal that this history is also the future. In this sense, the Baedeker stars construct a materially *explicit* idealisation of urban space that defines action in a way that reinforces the limits of that action.[9] Kracauer's series of points, on the other hand, construct an *implicit* space that depends on the vulnerability of the limits of that space to encourage discursive action. This vulnerability allows for the possibility of the space itself being reconfigured.

Kracauer's critique of traditional civic space does little to describe the relationship of the built metropolis to the more enigmatic socio-political definition of public space in post-Baedeker Berlin. Traditionally, squares, vistas, groups of buildings and perspective effects – material spaces orchestrated by planners – maintain the *appearance* of civicness by remaining constant, timeless, or, in a word, 'originary'. These planned spaces appear to stabilise the 'chaos' that modernity has wrought by disguising the city's supposed unruliness with unifying Baedeker stars: facades, colonnades, avenues, monuments and views. These are the traditional tools for shaping the polis, aesthetically as well as historically, socially and politically. Out of raw metropolitan space, they construct a civic Social Contract, bringing 'together what right permits and interest prescribes'.[10] To ensure their effectiveness as guardians of civil order, and to strengthen their ability to mask an amorphous modernity, these architectural devices gravitate toward homogeneity, fixity, and certainty – characteristics which are reinforced by the claim that they spring from some monolithic historical imperative.

Conversely, challenging the mandate of such an urban genealogy, weakens the certainty of enclosure on which the facade, the colonnade, the avenue, and the monument depend to frame civic space. Suspending these architectural devices' allegiance to a singular and absolute spatial lineage – releasing them from their obligation to reinforce a chosen history – allows them to be defined relative to one another, rather than to a fixed standard or origin. This multiple relativism redefines what 'right permits and interest prescribes' in fluid terms; homogeneity, fixity, and certainty are replaced by heterogeneity, flexibility, and potential.

Newness and regeneration

Since 1989, Berlin's civic leaders have organised three significant urban design competitions aimed at reconstructing the city: the Spreebogen, Reichstag and Spreeinsel competitions. Each of these competitions called for large-scale interventions or reconstructions within the city centre. The focus here will be on Berlin's 'stability directive' as illustrated in the Spreeinsel competition, which called for the design of four major programmatic components: a Federal Foreign Office, a Federal Ministry of the Interior, a conference centre, and a library. Totalling 271,100 square metres, the built area required by the programme is equivalent to a single building approximately one kilometre long, fifty metres wide, and six storeys tall.

According to the competition brief, these facilities were to be built on the Spreeinsel, an island in the 'heart' of the city. Much of Berlin's architectural history is located on this island, including the Altes Museum, the Cathedral, and the Palast der Republik. It is here that, as Berlin's Minister for Urban Development put it, 'the last phase in regenerating the historical centre of Berlin' would occur.[11] The notion of German 'regeneration' seems incongruous within the larger mythical formation of the European Union which, as noted above, is steeped in an aura of newness. Berlin's newness, stemming from a desire to define the city as the economic capital of unified Europe, has collided with Berlin's auto-regeneration as the national capital of unified Germany. The conflict deflects Berlin's future in two directions: regenerative nationalism and new transnationalism.

Regenerative nationalism

'Regenerative nationalism' expresses the competition organisers' desire to restore Berlin to its 'rightful' position at the centre of a unified Germany. In their eyes, unification made urgent the necessity to 'overcome a dual historical contradiction in the centre of Berlin'.[12] According to these planners and civic leaders, a capital city could only represent one national history. Because the Communist Palast der Republik, the former meeting hall of the GDR, did not reinforce their desired history, the brief required that this building be demolished. The ground on which it sits is essential to Berlin's imagined historical unity, for it also holds the memory of Andreas Schlüter's 17th century Stadtschloss (royal city palace) which was located on the same site. Exhuming the Stadtschloss, while simultaneously erasing the memory of the GDR, would fill in one of the most glaring gaps in Berlin's discontinuous history. Before its destruction during World War II, the Stadtschloss merited a Baedeker 'red star'; it established the Spreeinsel's symbolic authority as an administrative centre. The Palast der Republik, the GDR's *Volkskammer*, represents a very different red star, that of Communism. Prior to 1989, its gigantic halls were used for Party meetings whose echoing proceedings continued to fill the halls even in their often empty state. Echoing still, the Palast der Republik has become repulsive to West Berliners; it forms a kind of anti-gravity in the heart of the city, preventing Berlin from coalescing. Acknowledging the explosive possibilities still contained within this building, the competition brief diagnosed the Palast as cancerous in language running from the literal to the euphemistic. It cited a panel of experts who determined that the building contained asbestos. This contamination would make it difficult, they asserted, for the building ever to be safely occupied. Far more devastating than asbestos' tiny fibrous carcinogens, however, was the implicit poisoning of the ideological history of the GDR, a contamination which rendered it equally difficult to 'occupy' that ideology ever again. The degree to which this building's demolition was a political mandate, as opposed to a technical requirement, is readily apparent in the Spreeinsel jury's vehement opposition to one of the few competition entries that did refuse to remove the Palast der Republik: 'The preservation of the Palast der Republik on the grounds of its significance for 17 million people and the enclosure of the "negative space" of the Schloss . . . creates an unsatisfying spatial situation at the Lustgarten and on the Schlossplatz'.[13] The demolition of the Palast der Republik constituted, for these jurors, a justifiable euthanasia of the still potent strains of GDR ideology.

Clearly, GDR history has no value for these jurors' vision of Berlin's future. Equally clear is the degree to which that history's symbolic value necessitates its erasure. But erasure alone would not sufficiently define the city's urban future. Having expressed the need to 'excavate Berlin's historical grid', the Spreeinsel competition organisers also left no doubt that the 'correct grid' was defined by Schinkel in the early 19th century:

> It is anticipated that the participants in the competition will work with the historic city plan, not only with the many typologies of squares, spatial sequences, and green spaces, but also with the important buildings which have long characterised the urban image of central Berlin. Only a few relics remain of these.[14]

Acknowledging that most of this 'image of central Berlin' does not in fact exist – it never did – the organisers confess the extent to which the definition of Berlin's history is symbolic. When these planners use the term 'grid' to refer to Schinkel's organisation of urban space, they are also invoking the far-ranging 'grid' of his universal symbolic value; Schinkel *is*, in a sense, German architecture. Combining an exorcism of the Communists with the exhumation of Schinkel's largely unrealised plans for Berlin, the Spreeinsel competition's organisers hoped both to detach Berlin from GDR history, and to regenerate the capital's position within the redeployed history of an assumedly national architecture.

The Schinkel imperative hides a myriad of other, sometimes

problematic but equally important urban histories: postwar GDR planning; the 1930s Berlin of Albert Speer; Weimar Berlin; the Mietskaserne; Gründerzeit industrial developments; James Hobrecht's late-19th century Berlin; the 17th century Friedrichstadt plan; in short, that of Germany's long, varied, and unsuccessful struggle to determine an urban identity for its capital. To hide these histories is to hide the resonant possibilities of Kracauer's 'series of points'. The Palast der Republik is an ideologically charged point, a voice echoing across the discursive space of Marx-Engels Platz. Privileging Schinkel's history silences this echo.

New transnationalism

In counterbalance to the regenerative nationalism that has directed Berlin's planners to ground the city's future in an extant German soil, Berlin's new transnationalism demands that the city define itself as larger than German in order to find a position within the European Union. In 1989 the notion of a united Europe assumed enormous proportions: Europe would be the first outpost of the global village. These over-inflated hopes gave the Union an identity whose grandiosity was stretched into a frail utopian skin that barely concealed the volatile dangers now visible within Europe. As ruptures developed within the Union's overstretched hopes, Berlin's pan-European identity became increasingly difficult to define. In addition to the tumultuous shifts occurring in the ex-Eastern bloc, tears also developed because of the growth of nationalist tendencies in the West (particularly in France, Germany and Italy), the increasingly xenophobic European climate, and the aggressive protection of intra-European markets. How could Berlin define itself within the New Europe when Europe's mythical, trans-national newness was being punctured by the persistence of its jagged nationalisms?

Berlin subsequently responded to the European Union's indeterminate newness by emphatically reasserting its solidity, whether or not legitimate, and at any cost. In the Spreeinsel competition, the city excavated an urban model whose 'solidity' comes from a centralised expression of authority. In describing the winning scheme for the competition, the jury stated that 'the project takes an excellent approach to the historic topography . . . by placing a new, self-contained built volume on the site of the old Schloss, the project recreates the *spatial dominance of this place and effectively restores the centerpoint*'.[15] In its remarks, the jury was succinctly clear in defining the operative terms for the Spreeinsel: 'self-containment', 'restoration', 'dominance' and 'centrality'. The definitive character of these terms makes it clear that a number of Berlin's planners continue to efface an urbanism of potential through a strategy of prescriptive urban stability, leaving little space in the city for the 'unintentional', the 'fortuitous' and the 'emergent'.

Notes

1 Ignacio Ramonet, *Le Monde Diplomatique*, 487, Oct 1994, [author's translation].

2 Volker Hassemer, *Haupstadt Berlin – Stadtmitte Spreeinsel*, ed Felix Zwoch, Birkhäuser Verlag, (Berlin), 1994, pp6-7.

3 Inka Mülder, 'Erfahrendes Denken. Zu den Schriften Siegfried Kracauers vom Ersten Weltkrieg bis zum Ende der Weimarer Republik', dissertation, Tübingen University, 1984. Quoted by David Frisby in *Fragments of Modernity*, MIT Press, (Cambridge, Massachusetts), 1986, p135.

4 Siegfried Kracauer, 'Wiederholung', *Frankfurter Zeitung*, 29 May, 1932, trans David Frisby in *Fragments of Modernity*, MIT Press, (Cambridge, Mass), 1986, p141.

5 Siegfried Kracauer, 'The Cult of Distraction', *New German Critique*, Winter 1987, p93.

6 Siegfried Kracauer, 'Wiederholung', op cit.

7 Siegfried Kracauer, 'Berlin Landschaft', *Frankfurter Zeitung*, 10 Aug, 1931.

8 Nancy Fraser, 'Rethinking the Public Sphere – A Contribution to the Critique of Actually Existing Democracy" in *The Phantom Public Sphere*, ed. Bruce Robbins,

University of Minnesota Press, (Minneapolis), 1993, p17.

9 Squares, vistas, groups of buildings, and perspectival effects, as presented by Baedeker, require that there be an agreement about the city's identity and occupation, an agreement which also requires constant maintenance.

10 Jean-Jacques Rousseau, *The Social Contract*, trans Maurice Cranston, Penguin Books Ltd, (Middlesex), 1968, p49.

11 Volker Hassemer, op cit, p7.

12 Felix Zwoch, ed, *Haupstadt Berlin – Stadtmitte Spreeinsel*, op cit, p39.

13 Felix Zwoch, op cit, p62. Eventually, the jurors contradicted themselves by choosing a winning scheme that entirely enclosed the Schloss area.

14 Irmgard Schwaetzer, *Internationaler Städtebaulicher Ideenwettbewerb – Spreeinsel*, booklet sent to competition entrants, 1993, p2.

15 Unascribed comments of the jury, [author's italics], *Haupstadt Berlin – Stadtmitte Spreeinsel*, op cit, p49.

The City of Alexandrov
A study of proto-urban conditions and urban change.
Far right shows map of Alexandrov and surrounding area. Four distinct areas are outlined in which specific fields are examined.

Lake: Proto-urban Conditions
A Pastoral landscape of former marsh land. Presently urban development and deforestation is causing desiccation of the land. This is the place of memory for the victims of the last war, who died of starvation in besieged Leningrad (St Petersburg) and were buried here. One of the dynamic edges of the city (adjacent to a village) causing a conflict situation with the district of Vladimir. The city is acknowledging its recreational value and hopes to turn it into a park which as yet has been held back by the conflict between two striving forces: the urban development (City) and the village (District). Peripheral elements (uncontrolled dacha and garden plots) are taking over and the environmental value starts to deteriorate.

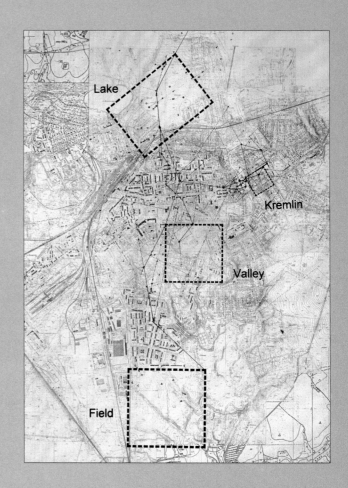

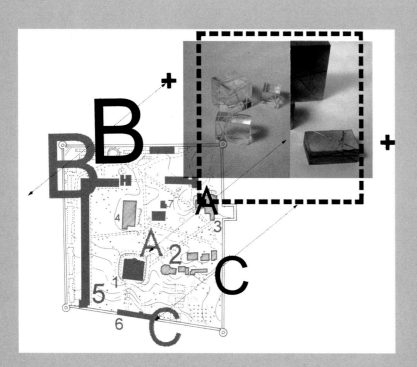

Kremlin: Micro-model
Established as a court by Ivan the Terrible, the Kremlin in Alexandrov once served as the centre of Russia. Though used as a museum by the city and as a cultural monument for tourism, the Russian Orthodox church is reclaiming the Kremlin as a convent. While the two parties fight for ownership, children, gypsies, tourists and the cattle-raising community also use it.

Micro-models are objects or processes found in the field. They are small-scale, compared to new processes being planned but share the same attributes or properties. It is possible to use smaller processes or objects to orchestrate larger changes.

In proto-urban fields existing local elements are often neglected but relate to older site conditions or to healthy native processes. Planning with micro-models ensures a certain continuity and particularity. Micro-models offer strategic means to establish new developments in urban areas.

Legend
A Occupants: territorial objects that move in the physical environment
1 convent 2 museum
B Attractors: players of the game
1 Russian Orthodox 2 City authority
C Users: migratory entities that interact with manifested elements
1 Children 2 Gypsies 3 Cattle-raising community 4 Tourists

CHORA
PROTO-URBAN CONDITIONS AND URBAN CHANGE
Raoul Bunschoten

Suturing the field

'Beyond the Revolution' indicates a field that has emerged in Europe containing a former wound, the Iron Curtain. CHORA is one of the many institutions that are emerging to tend this 'woundscape' and create sutures around it. A new research institute for architecture and urbanism, based in London, CHORA is a peripatetic agency working with a toolbox of comparative models, weaving different urban sites on both sides of the former divide and current edge of EC Europe. The main concern is the study of *proto-urban conditions*[1] – the ways in which they engender urban change and the management of this change. The following text briefly expands on these concerns and places them in the context of the changing urban context in Europe after 1989. CHORA has conducted research and developed projects in Linz, Austria, Helsinki, Finland and Alexandrov, Russia.[2] The current case study for Zagreb has been initiated by the city of Zagreb Bureau for Urban Planning and the Berlage Institute in Amsterdam.[3] A related project in Vladimir, with a grant from the European Community, is being conducted by the Academy of the Urban Environment, City of Vladimir and local residents.

Proto-urban conditions

In Eastern Europe changes have occurred that were unimaginable several years ago. After the initial euphoria a more complex side of the story is unfolding. The disappearance of repressive political systems and the partial destruction by war have created strong desires based on feelings of denial, neglect, resentment and outright hatred. The attempted phasing-out of a whole period of history creates equally strong myths related to older and easily manipulable periods. Territory becomes again a primal means of self-expression and the object of great disputes. Architecture and cities are the main icons of this expression. They are destroyed and rebuilt for similar objectives applied by opposite sides. A restless urbanism emerges which is fluid, anarchic and thirsty: thirsty for models, techniques, opportunities and, of course, a new culture of urban action. The restless energy that accompanies these developments has tremendous potential. What is this emerging urbanism and how can its potential be articulated and managed?

Enormous migratory movements of Russians from the former Soviet republics towards cities in Russia form one example for use of proto-urban conditions, or the tribal warfare, large population movements and radical 'ethnic cleansing' in the former Yugoslavia another. The emotions related to these phenomena are intense and on a collective scale are radical and momentous. The success of the development of urban environments in Central and Eastern Europe will strongly influence stability in Western and Central Europe. Consequently the EC is taking a keen interest in these developments by supporting innovative experiments in planning and restructuring. This concern for internal stability, combined with the desire of several 'fringe' states to join the EC and its possible expansion, makes the study of urban development in

places like Zagreb, Alexandrov and Vladimir a 'domestic' affair. These cities are models for the effects of proto-urban conditions. Zagreb is the capital city of a new state, Croatia, currently at war but with high hopes of becoming an EU member. Small Russian cities would seem to be of no interest from the perspective of Europe, but a change in urban culture in thousands of small towns will create democratic voting patterns in Russia and thus affect the political balance of Europe.

All cities are dynamic. The understanding of this dynamic nature, however, does not necessarily prepare us for emergent phenomena such as:

- a sudden loss of collective memory, of the structures of civic society and of the physical environment, caused by political revolutions or violent conflagrations;
- the (re)creation of new local or national identities;
- radically new economic spaces linked to information environments;
- wandering populations and 'soft' social structures that evolve gradually out of this population flux.

Evaluating the conditions underlying unpredictable changes will help us to describe their mechanics, while they are seemingly submerged they have a radical effect. Proto-urban conditions are like emotions in human beings; subliminal conditions that strongly affect physical states and behaviour. These conditions form a metaphoric emotive space in the city, a space which is in need of appropriate forms of expression. Contemporary planning discipline lacks these forms, and there needs to be an expansion or revision of the current practice. For example, a more culturally oriented form of planning should also use poetic modes of expression in order to come closer to the assumed nature of proto-urban conditions and understand better the value of their related phenomena. This revised discipline has to be exact in technique and in site-related fieldwork, mapping, and other forms of representation of urban environments, but profound in its reading of vectors of desire, modelling of values and use of their power of transformation.

Axiomatic sets and prototypes

Certain urban problems are derived from a malfunction of the exchange between the 'open' dynamic city and the 'submerged' proto-urban conditions. These conditions are constantly changing our environment towards new forms of urbanity. In order to employ these conditions to shape this urbanity, it is necessary to formulate methods that make them 'visible' and operational. CHORA is experimenting with techniques of simulation to affect proto-urban conditions, experiments that have so far involved inductive methods and prototype development with the use of an axiomatic set of four urban processes – *erasure, origination, transformation* and *migration* – forming operational 'fields'.[4] Each field contains one process in various forms. The intention of this exercise is to make it easier to read the 'handwriting' of any assumed proto-urban conditions in each field separately. The totality of fields simulates the given environment. In praxis the axiomatic set of fields assumes the characteristics of a specific urban environment. In the case studies conducted by CHORA the axiomatic set has increasingly related to geographic situations. In several projects the set begins to demonstrate possible structures for cultural planning by becoming a form of embedded narrative.

Folds

The management of urban change is dependent on the interaction of parties and structures which need anchoring in the physical environment. This occurs with the help of 'folds' in the urban fabric[5] under the influence of proto-urban conditions. In order to become part of operational planning they require the identification of: the proto-urban conditions; 'local authorities',[6] which anchor these conditions within existing institutions or places; actors, or participants with stated desires; and agents to develop the potential of growth in relation to the desires of actors.

Zagreb lies in a peripheral fold of the EC: Croatia hopes to enter the EC within the next few years. Zagreb itself is at the 'edge' of Europe, a gateway with both resisting and regulating functions. The forceful clarification of its boundaries (apart from the Eastern Slavonian territory, at the time of writing) with, as 'by-product', the exodus of almost all Croatian-Serbs is clearly meant to prepare Croatia for EC membership and bulwark or gateway status.

Zagreb, shifting identities

In 1617 a man is born in Zagreb, Yuri Krizhanich, he studied theology in Zagreb, then in Vienna, Bologna and Rome. In 1647 he visited Muscovy (now Russia) and became adviser to Tsar Alexis, assisting in the creation of the first schools and academies. After suspicions of spying he was sent into exile in Siberia where he wrote his 'Political Considerations', in which he tried to define the historical role of the new Muscovy. It is a programme for change based on a thorough reading of the life in Muscovy (it was the time of the first 'factory peasants'). As proto-Pan-Slav he called on Muscovy to rescue and unite all the stateless peoples – the Croats, Serbs, Bulgars, Czechs and Poles – and restore them to their national honour.

The Croatian state existed in various forms during the Middle Ages, but in 1527 Croatian noblemen elected the Habsburgs as rulers. This situation remained until January 1918 when the State of Slovenians, Croats and Serbs was founded, later the Kingdom of Yugoslavia.

On the day of the invasion of the German army into the Soviet Union, 22 June 1941, the Central committee of the Communist Party of Yugoslavia met and began preparatory discussions about armed resistance. The then Soviet Union was model and object of veneration and when Moscow gave the sign the prolonged and very tough struggle ensued which resulted in Tito and his partisans gaining power in Yugoslavia after the capitulation of the German army and those that sided with it.

On 25 June 1991 Croatia was proclaimed as a sovereign and independent state. On 22 May 1992 Croatia was accepted as a member of the UN.

Soon after its proclamation of independence war rages in parts of Croatian territory between the new Croatian forces and attacking forces of the former Yugoslav army, joined by Croatian Serbs.[7]

War and reconstruction

Division, war and destruction have changed the former Yugoslavia. Croatia is one of the nation-states emerging, with raw edges, scorched earth, its territory inhabited by seceding groups of people and an involvement in the war on another nation-state's territory. Towns and villages have been destroyed, institutions torn apart and old wounds opened. Under the umbrella of Europan several attempts were made in war-torn areas. It was emphasised that any reconstruction must not only take into account what existed before the 'imposition of the 50 years of the "revolutionary" rule'[8] but also needed to work with slow time-scales and scenarios on the basis of 'diagnostic maps'[9] which could take account of 'those structures which have been created "in an unplanned manner" as the time went by'.[10] This is in order not to reject all of the conditions of a certain period and engage in a more subtle form of destruction but to use the catastrophe to advantage and give form to uncharted but significant entities.

Zagreb, the old and new capital of Croatia, was not touched much by the war physically but is now struggling to construct normality: to reconcile 40 years of 'second city' (denied city) status in a Communist State, with new ambitions as capital, and to plan for a future aimed at assimilation with Western Europe. A 'search for [the] identity of a Croatian metropolis' is introduced by Slavko Dakic, in his essay 'Metropolitan Identity of Zagreb'[11] where he states that their aim is to achieve an exemplary status for Zagreb in Europe by pursuing dynamic systems of planning that achieve 'sustainable' development. This term refers to the reconciliation of development and environmental issues, of the quality of life of one generation and the processes that ensure the preservation of the global environment.

'Soft' structures, turbo environments and sustainability

Europan's workshops in war-damaged areas of Croatia have raised the issue of uncharted but significant structures created 'in an unplanned manner'. How to diagnose these 'soft' structures and how to employ them? Slavko Dakic's hopes for Zagreb's 'sustainable' development imply a delicately balanced dynamic environment which has much in common with other micro-urban regions in other cities in Europe. But Zagreb is a 'turbo-environment':[12] it is the capital of a state at war, and part of a struggle in which nationalities and religious entities are pitted against one another; while also entering a new economic sphere of influence with its own highly competitive dynamics. Its forced segregation between nationalities and religions is in contradiction to the powerful heterogeneity of modern urban metropolises. The sustainability that is needed is one that links the regulation of the raw forces of such a volatile environment to the maintenance of a structure of change that resists homogeneity and that creates the basis for urban environments that are not defined by national boundaries and interests.

The 'Frames of the Metropolis' workshop[13] speculated on planning strategies for a central zone in Zagreb. This zone, a large and very sensitive 'fold' in Zagreb's urban fabric has great potential. The issues emerging can be grouped into four categorical frames derived from the axiomatic sets described above, similar to those developed by CHORA for the project *Linzer Entfaltungen*[14] in Linz and Gateway in Helsinki. These groups are autonomously defined but have to interact:
• preservation based on the proximity of the older part of Zagreb, and a concern for ecology (ecology is becoming a collective concern, both concrete and near-spiritual, a link

for collective memory and nature on a global scale, a new common good);

- the creation of new public space as cultural instrument of change to promote the status of Zagreb as capital city and as central European metropolis in line with Helsinki, Berlin, Vienna, Bratislava and Athens;
- urban trading floors as engines of change that are ahead of economic developments and create a real gateway situation in terms of an intensification of flows and networks; regulated trade with surrounding countries is an imperative in addition to an information environment that enables active global exchange;
- mobility and democratic reform; the modes for this range from innovative use of the inner-city railway line to EC investments in municipal policy and the institutional development of strategic and cultural planning prototypes that create civic action and cohesion.

Unfolding

Strategic and cultural planning involve scenarios that link economic and demographic changes to factors such as identity, culture, history and collective memory. These factors are often expressed with narrative or other means that do not easily mix with more seemingly exact methods. In a volatile environment moving towards a fully-fledged democracy, large-scale urban transformations cannot be implemented without forms of planning and management of the subsequent changes that resemble 'game' structures. These consist of new institutional structures that include radically different partners, agents and actors. These structures have a temporal development of negotiated planning built in, which allows for an 'unfolding' of planning scenarios that are able to react to changing interests and situations. This is an essential requirement in the context of Eastern Europe where societies are in an unpredictable flux and any fixed strategies will be outdated immediately.

Alexandrov: agitating models

'There are two Russian nations: the immense provincial-village heartland, and an entirely disparate minority in the capital, alien to it in thought and Westernised in culture.' Solzhenitsyn suggests that the impulse [to evolve to full nationhood] must come from the local productive economy and from locally elected government. He wants a moral revolution, one of self-limitation, and the central government is poorly suited to creating it.[15]

Similar to other regional cities in Russia, Alexandrov was planned in various stages by State policy and was run by central State bureaucracies combined with a local Party apparatus. Alexandrov and its surroundings have the makings of a micro-region but will eventually become drawn into the immediate spheres of influence exerted by Moscow and Vladimir. Alexandrov's industry has recently undergone a change from a State-controlled defence industry to one struggling for something to do, being virtually at a stand-still. This change has caused a catastrophic disruption in the fabric of the city and its structures, leaving in its wake a period of transition in which the former functions of the city require redefinition. Currently Alexandrov attempts to fill this void by posing itself as a magnet, or attractor, for new technological industries and for cultural activities. It must compete with the whole region and neighbouring cities, and guard against the terrifying odds of a collapsed national infrastructure and wide-

spread corruption and highway crime. Alexandrov is entering an increasingly global condition which is inherently dynamic and subject to complex changes in economic, political and social changes, often beyond the city's immediate regulatory capacity. The effects of this global relation are manifested locally in Alexandrov in ways which follow complex behaviour patterns, especially visible boundary conditions. These boundary conditions demonstrate self-regulatory behaviour or reveal characteristics that point to the emergence of new identities. The self-regulatory behaviour forms a kind of 'awareness' or 'consciousness' of an environment. This crystallises into an emergence of cultural forms of expression. It is here that identities at odds with existing ones, (or identities which are only in the process of being assembled) are sketched out. A technology of simulation and interaction should therefore describe this non-linear self-regulatory behaviour but also simulate and propose formations of public space. The models establish three frames within which relatively simple sets of rules for interaction can be set. The value of such models lies in the potential prediction of new emergent forms, but also in the possible provision of additional or alternative solutions to a planned change and to provide guide-lines for the implementation of some of these extra situations.

Common to thousands of other cities in central and northern Russia, the city of Alexandrov is undergoing a transformation of its social environment where the preceding structure is no longer the most significant factor in determining the future. As a model case study Alexandrov can contribute to the gradual redevelopment of Russian cities, and deserves a longer period of study. Observation is an interactive mechanism which has already had an effect in the instruction and confidence-bolstering of the chief architect and his team, and other participants.

CHORA's work in Alexandrov is the result of an earlier co-operation between Raoul Bunschoten and Vyacheslav Glazychev in 1990:[16] 'The Skin of the Earth' was exhibited during the events that led towards the final break-up of the Soviet Union, a process it modelled. The relationship was revived when Raoul Bunschoten and Robert Mull, then both unit masters at the AA, held a joint workshop at the Moscow Institute of Architecture in 1993. By then Glazychev had founded the AUE and was conducting fieldwork and urban planning projects in smaller towns in Russia. The founding of CHORA made it possible to initiate a collaboration with the AUE.

Prototypes, urban devices and form

Prototypes and techniques of unfolding and embedding are needed to create 'public space' in a strategic planning process. Prototypes are vectors of desire, creating the necessity to bring parties together to decide upon the urban device to implement or 'map' the device onto more complex situations. A device is an organisational structure which becomes visible in the urban fabric as form. CHORA has experimented with this set of urban tools in Linz and is preparing their use in Alexandrov. The first field session in the city of Alexandrov conducted by CHORA and members of the AA produced data which will be further developed in a second session in 1996. These involve a second axiomatic set of themes: urban icon formation, resonance and micro-models.

Action and Simulation

Town planning and urban culture are political concerns and as the conditions that generate urban change in Eastern Europe are

Valley: Urban Icon

Public space recurs as a product of interaction within culture in a particular spatial or organisational form, creating collective memory. Encoded in the object of public space this memory germinates collective identity. Urban icons, a masque or second skin of public space, express collective identity. As such they actively support the development of the society by increasing the interests and potential of individuals in interaction. To guarantee continuity of the public domain in proto-urban areas, icon-forming needs to have a describing and prescribing function as communicative ground and generative form.

The distinctive landscape is a river basin forming a precious green open space in the city. Urban planning since Katherine the Great, has left its legacies in present street patterns and land uses. These impositions uniformly disregard the topography and neighbourhood of this area. Several urban institutions identified around the area provide a potential network for unfolding the neighbourhood.

Legend
A *Environment: actual geography of valley landscape*
B *Local Authorities: that provide intensifications of networks*
C *Animators: local experts or actors*
D *Agents: external experts*
E *Public Masque (Landscape): the alternative skin that supports self-organisation*
F *Frame: legal frame to anchor and support products of interaction*

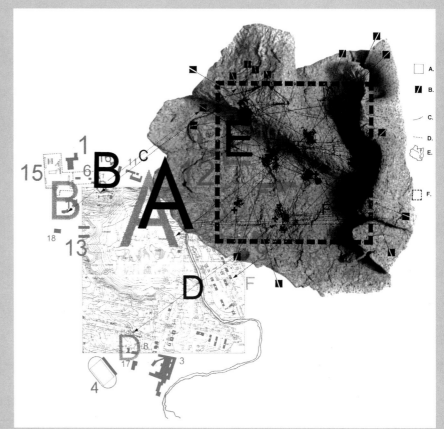

Field: Resonant Pattern

The former city edge is marked by high-rise housing, typical of the Soviet period, facing towards the open space and the forest. Here, construction of a co-operative apartment, for Russian refugees returning from other republics, is destroying the village occupying the same site. The political transformation of Russia enables people to possess private land on which they can build a dacha. On the weekend there is a steady flow of pedestrian traffic from the city into the woodland where the private housing colony is rapidly growing.

Legend
A *A large number of the returning Russian population is not allowed to settle within a 100 kilometre radius of Moscow. Satellite cities like Alexandrov are now exposed to a great demand for new housing for these people.*
B *The rural structure of collective farming is under pressure from the influx of products from the EC and also from expanding cities like Alexandrov.*
C *Virtually no factory has survived the political change of recent years because of competition with foreign products. Currently the West is investing substantial capital in the East in order to prevent the flux of migration and stabilise the population by creating jobs.*
D *State investment on large-scale infrastructures has been suspended while individuals are busy constructing their own sheds on garden plots.*

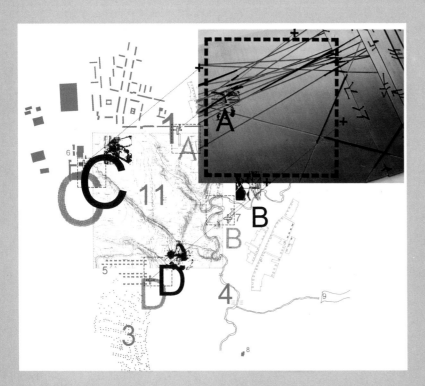

largely new and very difficult to understand, there is an urgent need for exemplary studies. The aims of these studies can be divided into three categories:
- to aid local populations in their quests for direct action, direct democracy, self-determination and self-organisation;
- to contribute directly to the decision-making process of authorities with the help of demonstrations and simulations, and to train authorities in the possibilities of the first aim;
- to create models and prototypes for other Eastern European cities and towns, and for the urban planning discipline.

Gonchary, Vladimir

Simulation is the implementation of an alternative reality as action into an actual environment. In Vladimir, Vyacheslav Glazychev and the AUE have, with the Vladimir city planning authorities, conducted a series of workshops which focused on the neighbourhood of Gonchary. The workshops examined the general situation of neglect, decline and lack of urban structure in a typical inner-city low intensity area, between the famous cathedral of the 11th century, the former main gate (the Golden Gate) to the city and the busy train lines along the river. Gonchary has an older population, which is divided between those who want to leave and those who want to improve their surroundings. There are no municipal facilities, industry or newcomers.

Glazychev set up a task force of experts from Vladimir and Moscow, with visiting specialists from Britain, Switzerland and Germany, with no certainty that he could draw in the population. However, he succeeded by arousing curiosity: people came in slowly, almost one by one, and he quickly made them appropriate the particular parts of the project by proposing and taking care of problems or initiatives; a slow and fragile process in an environment where there is enormous lethargy and few decision-

making skills, a legacy of life under a system that discouraged people from taking individual action. At the end of the workshop a Territorial Development Corporation was agreed upon, local committees were activated, Gonchary became an official model for the other neighbourhoods in Vladimir, the city of Vladimir officially committed itself to various projects, and the AUE was commissioned to further guide and advise the city and the neighbourhood.

The AUE is undertaking four actions. Each of these actions constructs an aspect of simulation and action, each is a part of a demonstrative and possible reality:
- AUE as a *migrating body* (invited from the outside by local authorities or groups) has a form of institutional legitimacy;
- AUE acts as an *agent*, drawing out hidden social structures, dreams and desires; using these networks of connections it finds out things that are unknown to the legitimate authorities. The agent's action of 'weaving' connects two disparate realms (ephemeral or 'soft' entities and institutional bodies) and can turn a void into a mediating space.
- the AUE acts as *masque*, as a catalyst of a narrative space; it becomes a vehicle of emotive expression within a newly initiated cultural context; its creation of maps and historical research brings ephemeral or forgotten conditions to the surface as potential cultural assets.
- The actions of the AUE catalyse but also simulate the construction of a neighbourhood as a *symbolic home*; this becomes a positive attractor in the city as a whole; a model that borrows from other, older traditions.

Very consciously Glazychev hopes to create a quasi-autonomous organism while simultaneously creating an education for local authorities and a potential threshold space for involvement of these authorities in locally initiated affairs.

Notes

1 A term coined by CHORA, after a first test run in Diploma Unit 2 of the Architectural Association (AA), London.

2 The projects were in co-operation with: Linz, the City of Linz; Helsinki, with the University of Arts and Design and the City of Helsinki; and Alexandrov, with the City of Alexandrov, members of the AA, London, and the Academy of the Urban Environment (AUE), in Moscow, headed by Vyacheslav Glazychev. Funding has been provided by the *Stimuleringsfonds voor Architectuur* and the *Stichting Fonds voor Beeldende Kunsten, Vormgeving en Bouwkunst*, both in the Netherlands.

3 Raoul Bunschoten is currently guest professor at the Berlage Institute in Amsterdam.

4 In a dynamic environment it is important to allocate layers of processes or sets of forms belonging to a certain agent or form. The aim is to allocate different frames of analysis to the urban environment under study. Any kind of regulation or proposed implementation may then be directed at such layers or sets.

5 This word has been recently overused but since this fashion has left it behind, it can be restored to being a useful metaphor.

6 Michel de Certeau, *The Practise of Everyday Life*, University of California Press, (London), 1988.

7 Lionel Kochnan and Richard Abraham, *The Making of Modern Russia*, by Penguin Books, (London), 1986.

8 Part of Article 2, *Europan Croatia*, (Croatia), 1994.

9 Mladen Skreblin, 'Language of the Patterns, Theses on Soft Method and Organisation of Reconstruction', *Europan Croatia*, (Croatia), 1994.

10 Ibid.

11 Slavko Dakic, 'Metropolitan Identity of Zagreb' and introduction, *Zagreb/Govor o Gradu*, Bureau for Development Planning and Environmental Protection in Zagreb, (Zagreb), 1995. Dakic is the Director of the Bureau.

12 Turbo-environments are environments that are propelled into new states of existence hardly imaginable a short while ago. They may appear in primal or raw form pushed by forces, political, economic, of near-demonic nature that emerge in a society that is being pulled apart by geopolitical developments. In other places there may be mere turbulence and only a desire to evaluate the erratic movements and wandering population, to gain some kind of control or guiding function.

13 'Frames of the Metropolis', a joint workshop held jointly by the City of Zagreb and the Berlage Institute, organised by Vedran Mimica of the Berlage, was held in June 1995.

14 See *Linzer Entfaltungen*, 'Artifice', (London), October 1995, and 'Archis', (Amsterdam), February 1996, also in preparation in book form, Vienna, 1996.

15 Geoffrey Hosking, 'Mother Russia's Prophet Returns', *The Independent*, 21 Sept 1995, a review of the book, *The Russian Question at the End of the Twentieth Century*, Harvill Press, (London), 1995.

16 'The Skin of the Earth, a Dissolution in Fifteen Parts', which Glazychev courageously agreed to hold, as an official of the Union of Architects of the former Soviet Union, was a project conceived for, and exhibited in, the main exhibition hall of the society, in Moscow. Main collaborators were Alain Chiaradia, currently a trustee of CHORA, and Kristina Kotov, assisted by a team of young architects. For publication see *A+U*, no 263, Sept 1992, or *B*, no 49, (Denmark), 1992.

RON KENLEY

ARC

The weapon, the line, the wall and the hole – A DADA Project[1]

The bend of some lines
   around a point
    available
the wind with the odour of oil and bromide
each object draws a letter   *and I write letters*
the abyss   *tiredness cut into letters*
observation post   *the station on the map*
of precision in the wait
I stuck the stamp laced with blood deep as dawn
contours colours explosions cries twist and fix
the mottled verb is red the mottled word birds flying low stained with oil
flying towards the sail
      the mottled word draws the alphabet [2]

Coincidences make
In January 1989, an essay by Dominique Noguez, titled 'LENINE dada' is published in Paris. It traces a fictional while profound link between the DADA movement and the Russian Revolution based on the coincidence in Zurich of Lenin and the DADA founders. At least two of the movement's founders were Romanian, Tristan Tzara and Marcel Janco.

By the end of the same year, Prague had its 'Velvet Revolution', the Berlin Wall was pierced and Nicolae Ceausescu, the Romanian dictator was dead.

A particularity of most, if not all of these political changes was the active participation (in their early days) of poets, writers, actors, dramatists, architects. Václav Havel, (author and playwright) is the President of the Czech Republic; in Bucharest, Ion Caramitru (actor and director), Ana Blandiana and Mircea Dinescu (poets) were all included in the first government. More significant for the present essay is the role played by the architects. The Institute of Architecture *Ion Mincu,* is the home of both the School of Architecture in Bucharest and of the Romanian Union of Architects. Between December 1989 and June 1990, the Institute had the geographical privilege of location in the heart of the political ferment and events that took over the city's University Square in the turmoil of change. Today, almost six years on, monuments, flowers and graffiti mark the actions and reactions that span between protest and its eventual violent dissolution through the action of the miners invading the site of the four month demonstration and the Institute of Architecture itself.

the project – its construction
The coincidences of historical record matter. They are gathered in memory better than in archives. And memory inhabits. This essay attempts to bring together a variety of sources which might be of use for an architecture 'beyond the Wall'. The technique of presentation is akin to collage more than to the development of a sequence. Every piece contains at least a direct reference to an architectural device. The familiar terminology will help, but only on condition that it be re-evaluated in its new context.

In the construction of the text, synonymous to the project hinted at here, particular attention is paid to crossings of an uneasy kind (intellectual thought and politics, art and action, holes and places, programme and fiction, contradiction and hope). They constitute the best illustrations of a reading of Bucharest as it was left beyond 1989, as well as the germs for the new projects that will take over the city.

The resulting assemblage may be read as notes towards a project. It is certainly not definitive, but hopefully engaging. Narrative continuity may be present, but it is more like the rambling of thought that finds new turns and unexplored rooms, echoing the steps of the same sound. It is in the use of the architectural devices of drawing in projections with lines, picking or making points, erasing, measuring, adding, accommodating and so on that an architectural project comes into being. I hope this will be the destiny of the one I fictionally hint to here.

The Zone is not a place[3]
A few minutes walk away from University Square, a different and possibly more powerful presence of architectural politics is visible: the Zone. Demolished and hurriedly rebuilt, in so many ways unfinished for better or worse.

 Let the accountants count the waves
 let others shake the keys
 be the crow with the violin, the madman, the porter
 who in December carries glue to the trees.[. . .]
 And instead of rest choose pepper
 so you can salute if it's not too bad
 those who put concrete, glass and steel girders
 in the space from which God has fled [4]

The Boulevard of the Victory of Socialism (originally), renamed the Union Boulevard, begins at its western end with the House of the People, renamed the House of Parliament, while opening in the opposite direction to the horizon of large roundabouts and ever-extending half-finished facade blocks.[5] The House of the People is itself an unfinished project, but it is used both for parliamentary sessions and to show any visitors the monumental achievement it represents in volume, craftsmanship and materials. Work on the rest of the projects is advancing at a slow pace and the entire Zone is still a hole on the map of the city, six years after the fall of the regime that produced it.

the hole of an open solution
Slavoj Zizek begins his *Critique of Ideology* with a reference to the Romanian flag:

 The most sublime image that emerged in the political upheavals of the last years – and the term sublime is to be conceived here in the strictest Kantian sense – was undoubtedly the unique picture from the time of the violent overthrow of Ceausescu in Romania: the rebels waving the national flag with the red star, the Communist symbol, cut out, so that instead of the symbol standing for the organising principle of the national life, there was nothing but a hole in its centre.[6]

Zizek introduces the image as representative of an 'open' situation, when the old order having lost its hegemonical power has not yet been replaced by the new one:

> ... and what really matters is that the masses who poured into the streets of Bucharest 'experienced' the situation as 'open', that they participated in the unique intermediate state of passage from one discourse (social link) to another, when, for a brief, passing moment, the hole in the big Other, the symbolic order, became visible.

Here the system of the social link was suspended as the hole was cut, allowing and demanding the intellectual reflection and occupying both the place of the hole and the time, *all the time*. Zizek continues:

> The enthusiasm which carried them was literally the enthusiasm over this hole, not yet hegemonised by any positive ideological project; all ideological appropriations (from the nationalistic to the liberal-democratic) entered the stage afterwards and endeavoured to 'kidnap' the process which originally was not their own.

The historical moment of change was marked by the hole on the flag. It was of course sewn together fairly quickly, but surely this is not the only hole to need mending.

The hole and the wall

After the flag, the architecture and the city are left with the hole.

> *hole, wall, face and landscape construct*

A hole (black) implies a wall (white). A 'white wall/black hole' system is a face. I take Gilles Deleuze and Félix Guattari as a guide and major reference to this essay. The open system of their *A Thousand Plateaux* suits the rambling of thought writing the programme of this project. The multiplicity and precision of reference moving with ease between disciplines and crossing at points that allow the anchoring of the argument is most appropriate in the examination of the relationship of Power building walls and the force affirming its opposition in piercing them . . .

> A broad face with white cheeks, a chalk face with eyes cut in for a black hole. Clown head, white clown, moon-white mime, angel of death, Holy Shroud. The face is not an envelope exterior to the person who speaks, thinks, or feels . . . A child, woman, mother, man, father, boss, teacher, police officer, does not speak a general language but one whose signifying traits are indexed to specific faciality traits. Faces are not basically individual; they define zones of frequency or probability, delimit a field that neutralises in advance any expressions or connections unamenable to the appropriate significations.[7]

This system stratifies or forms matter. Further, the face correlates landscape. 'Architecture positions its ensembles – houses, towns or cities, monuments or factories – to function like faces in the landscape they transform.'[8] From and beyond face and landscape manuals of Christian education, the arts adopted and disseminated the correlation. In painting, the landscape is posi-

FROM ABOVE: In Bucharest, the bronze statue of Lenin is lowered; the President orders the demolition; maquette of the Boulevard for the Victory of Socialism.

tioned as a face treating one like the other; film uses close-up both to deal with face as landscape and to define film as black hole and white wall, screen and camera. 'So, is your mother a landscape or a face? A face or a factory? (Godard) . . .'[9]

fiction

Imagination allows the possibility of *fiction*. I am using the term as the potential for imaginative synthesis, bringing together or arching over that which happened in order to unfold in time as a story.

Lines of fiction

three kinds of line

A story divides the living present into describable instants. Describable with actions or movements through space. Time and space united and interdependent, substitute one for the other.

'each object draws a letter/the mottled word draws the alphabet'[10]

The lines of writing, flesh, life, luck or misfortune and so on present in the construction of fiction determine a rigid, supple segmentarity, but also the possibility of flight that denies the segmental qualities of the other lines.

Constructing with lines a face in the landscape of the city is the domain of the architect. In contemporary Bucharest, the three lines (scalar, vector and abstract) have a political dimension (in which centrality and segmentarity contain and enable each other through the mechanisms of hierarchy). But they carry also inherent dangers: fear, clarity, power, disgust or passion for abolition.

political dimensions: fear, clarity, power, disgust

Fear undermines the segmental quality or determination of the line. The fear of loss of the status quo, the de-stabilising of the structure of fixed reference petrifies:

> The values, morals, fatherlands, religions and private certitudes our vanity and self-complacency generously grant us are so many abodes the world furnishes for those who think on that account that they stand and rest amid stable things; they know nothing of the enormous rout they are heading for . . . *in flight from flight.*[11]

Clarity is obtained in the distinctions observed in fullness, the holes that appear in the compact and in subsidiary segmentation, encroachment, overlapping, migrations. The result of the variations, the suppleness apparently gained is translated into 'the system of petty insecurities that leads everyone to their own black hole in which to turn dangerous, possessing a clarity on their situation, role and mission even more disturbing than the certitudes of the first line.'[12]

> Power acts on both scalar and vector lines simultaneously.
> Every man of power jumps from one line to the other, alternating between a petty and a lofty style, the rogue's style and the grandiloquent style, drugstore demagoguery and the imperialism of the high-ranking government man. But this whole chain and web of power is immersed in a world of mutant flows that eludes them. It is precisely this impotence that makes power so dangerous. The man of power will always want to stop the lines of flight . . . by creating a void . . . This is what takes place in the artificial conditions of totalitarianism or the 'closed vessel'.[13]

disgust

In a lecture on Dada held in 1924, Tristan Tzara described the beginnings of the Movement:

> The beginnings of Dada were not the beginnings of an art, but of a disgust. Disgust with the magnificence of philosophers who for 3000 years have been explaining everything to us (what for?), disgust with the pretensions of these artists-God's-

representatives-on-earth, disgust with passion and with real pathological wickedness where it was not worth the bother; disgust with a false form of domination and restriction *en masse* . . . disgust with all the catalogued categories . . . disgust with the lieutenants of a mercantile art made to order according to a few infantile laws, disgust with the divorce of good and evil, the beautiful and the ugly . . . From all these disgusts, may I add, it draws no conclusion, no pride, no benefit.[14]

It may be useful to retain some of the terms used by Tzara: disgust, passion, destruction. And to point to a link between the Dada movement and the Russian Revolution. Efros wrote in *Sovremennyi Zapad* in 1923 under the title 'Dada': ' "Let everyone shout: there is a great destructive, negative work to be accomplished. To sweep, to clean", that was achieved by Russia with the Revolution.'[15]

Disgust or the passion for abolition is acting on the abstract lines of flight. Desire or passion is by definition assembled or assembling. Any assemblage depends on rationality and efficiency on the one hand, but also on the passions it brings into play, the desires that play a constitutive part in both senses: they constitute, but are also constituted in the assemblage. Desire, or passion cannot desire its own repression.

> The masses certainly do not passively submit to power; nor do they 'want' to be repressed, in a kind of masochistic hysteria; nor are they tricked by an ideological lure . . . Desire is never an undifferentiated instinctual energy, but itself results from a highly developed, engineered set-up rich in interactions: a whole supple segmentarity that processes molecular energies and potentially gives desire a fascist determination.[16]

when the line of flight becomes a line of death

It is not enough for the line of flight, of flesh or of writing to cross the wall, to get out of the black hole; it needs to connect with other lines and grow with them. If instead it turns to destruction, to the passion of abolition, it turns into a line of death.

The town and the State

If the hole lined with buildings in the centre of Bucharest is an architectural construct of totalitarianism, how is it so?

Totalitarianism is a state affair concerning the relationship between the State as an assemblage and the system that maintains the security of a status quo in *values, morals, fatherlands, religions and private certitudes.*[17] It is therefore profoundly conservative. In that sense, the totalitarian state is defensive and acts by the appropriation of the military apparatus. Not to wage war, but to exert constant and disciplinary control over all aspects of the organisation of society. (Note the passion for *uniform* so characteristic of such regimes in dress, parading movement, planning, production or construction). At its extreme, the danger is in the destructive acts; those are not a way to progress through erasure and replacement, but to merely remove that which is in the way whether natural, material or spiritual.

circulation and circuits

What is the relationship between the town and the State? Firstly, the town and the road, exchange, network and the local administration of rules or laws, including those regulating exchange of all sorts.

> The town is the correlate of the road. The town exists only as a function of circulation and of circuits; it is a remarkable point on the circuits that create it, and which it creates. It is defined by entries and exits; something must enter it and exit from it. It imposes a frequency. It effects a polarisation of matter, inert, living or human; it causes the phylum, the flow to pass through specific places, along horizontal lines.

It is a phenomenon of *transconsistency*, a *network*, because it is fundamentally in contact with other towns.[18]

Urban compositions

traces: cardo and decumanus

For Bucharest, the new town in the Zone (1977-89) had its main road, the Boulevard for the Victory of Socialism, laid to become a new *decumanus maximus*. It is crossed at a right angle by the Bratianu Boulevard, the continuation of the 1930s north-south axis which in turn completed a Hausmann-inspired construction in a modern idiom. At its eastern end, a roundabout distributes to the north-east through the Decebal Boulevard and to the south-east through the Burebista Boulevard. Both names refer to ancient leaders, one known through his ability to bring prosperity and geographical extent, the other for heroically defending the national entity against Roman invaders. The implication is that westwards up the Unirii (Union) Boulevard, the advance is through political and historically indexed time, not merely space. There is a major difference between the Magheru buildings (1930s) and the Unirii project (1977-89).

projections

It is as if the former was designed in *axonometric* and the latter in *perspective*; in one the volumetric enclosure is articulated, in the other, the axial viewing is revealed or hidden.

axonometric and collage

The 1930s' buildings abandon the symmetry of composition as a device, demonstrably taking over the space of the boulevard and of the adjacent streets by negotiation and thus in opposition to the Hausmannian ethic that generated the boulevard in the first place (adjacent ownership, facade height restrictions, horizontal continuity down the boulevard, at crossroads and corners). They were primarily collective dwellings, but their form attests to the development of diversity in organisation, adapting and articulating different and changing local conditions within a general dynamic of the city (at the scale of the boulevard). Furthermore, the buildings achieved an intensity of occupation that makes the overall composition. These buildings as an ensemble do not respond merely to the discipline of axonometric volumes as a way to construct their enclosure; they allow and encourage collage to build and be built within the circuits that determine the town.

connections and flexibility

The interior ordering device, the apartment, was developed 'around a central nucleus of generous dimensions, consisting of a living room in direct connection with the other rooms, this connection being the element of the dwelling's flexibility.'[19]

in interiors

Through the interior, we connect to the Dada as avant-garde. More precisely to Tzara declaring: 'What interests a Dadaist is his own mode of life.'[20]

The link to the collective dwellings of the early 30s in Bucharest is provided by Marcel Janco, Dada founder, painter, architect, writer:

Man builds for the sole purpose of creating an interior for himself, Architecture is only the art of seeing in space. There is a space limited by planes, walls – *the interior* – and, as a result of the interior, the volume, *the exterior*. The power of creation of architecture rests in the attitude of seeing in space, of conceiving the limited space and of drawing from it all consequences in the exterior volume. The modern interior gives proportions to the height and size of the rooms according to the purpose.[21]

FROM ABOVE: The city behind the wall; external ornament on the House of the People; unfinished work in Bucharest; the blind man lost. All images taken from the film Architecture and Power *by Augustin Ioan.*

Perspective and symmetries

If, as Janco writes, 'Architecture is only the art of seeing in space', and if the Magheru Boulevard is developed in an axonometric way of seeing space, we should now turn towards the perspective employed in the composition of the Unirii (ex-Socialist Victory) Boulevard. One striking characteristic of the plan, is the unifying effort to achieve symmetry.

symmetries in perspective

The single-point perspective relies on bilateral or reflective symmetry. This, as Robin Evans pointed out in his analysis of the reconstruction of Mies' Barcelona Pavilion[22] is the kind of symmetry that architects mainly use. It excludes other kinds of symmetry: that which can exist in a principle, Vitruvius' more general concept, Hambidge's 'dynamic symmetry', or mathematical varieties, such as rotational symmetry. A closer look reveals the physical and conceptual thinness of this approach – even the eastern end of the composition gets distributed beyond the roundabout to the north-east through the Decebal Boulevard and to the south-east through the Burebista Boulevard, at right angles to each other, despite any physical or visual topographic effect. It is revealing that the planimetric considerations were given priority over the complex that the city was and were extended beyond the optical effect that generated them in the first place.

distraction as displacement

Referring to Kant's concept of aesthetic judgement, Evans concludes: 'Oblivious to the tremors that beset the present, we intimate a pattern for a potential future. *Distraction is not amnesia, it is displacement.*'[23]

Let us recall the physical displacement of eight Bucharest churches – the term used was 'translation' as part of the Boulevard project. Some retained their address, but changed location which implies that streets were also moved or retraced, others simply had to change address.

Such acts of substitution and replacement are found in the roles and actions described by Tzara in 'How I became charming, congenial and delicious':

> There are people (journalists, lawyers, amateurs, philosophers) who maintain even the other forms: business, marriages, visits, wars, diverse conferences, joint-stock companies, politics, accidents, dances, economic crises, nervous breakdowns, just for variations of dada.[24]

equivalence not privilege

The mechanism of bilateral symmetry in the planimetric and perspectival construction of the Boulevard distracts from the centrality it was supposed to point towards and the unity of timeless space it was meant to represent. Robin Evans clarifies this:

> It is generally believed that bilateral symmetry asserts unity by emphasising the centre. Monumental architecture has been demonstrating this for millennia . . . The social order of theocracy, tyranny and aristocracy seems locked into this formal arrangement . . . The transformation of bilateral symmetry in monumental architecture is a spectacular instance of the mute politics embodied in appearances. When we have rid ourselves of the prejudices established over the centuries by means of architecture, we may recognise that bilateral symmetry is a way of creating equivalence, not privilege.[25]

There are two readings that Robin Evans' analysis offers for the Union Boulevard and its buildings.

distraction from destruction

The first is to do with the distraction from destruction. The destruction of the synaptic connections between buildings, streets and the city, whether through demolition or displacement was legitimised in State thinking by the power of the distraction; the architecture that was to replace the old city could only be the architecture of forgetting. As Evans warns us, forgetting is a social activity. Ignorance, as much as knowledge, can be constructed socially. 'The collective practice of forgetting produces innocence – the kind that we construct to protect ourselves from others, and others from ourselves, not the kind that is lost.'[26]

limits of classical symmetry

The second is about the limitations of symmetry in the classical sense, the kind applied pretty literally in the Bucharest of 1989: 'Symmetry is what we see at a glance, based on the fact that there is no reason for any difference, and based also on the face of a man: whence it happens that *symmetry is only worked in breadth, not in height or depth.*'[27]

From place to non-place and back again – a proposal

intensity of programme and organisation of form

The hope for the new town resides in what happens or may happen behind the facade of the thin walls of symmetry and perspective. The intensity rather than density of programme and organisation of form may be realised through the process of adaptation of whatever is already there, rather than the imagination of what might replace it.

the tension between town and State

The project will only work within the tension existing between town and State. This tension is generated by the States hierarchical, subordinating system that stratifies and extends across the horizontal lines in depth. It makes the geographic, ethnic, linguistic, moral, economic technological points resonate within the diversity of order they each present. The elements identified in the analysis throughout this essay (lines, directions, intersections, points, projections) are familiar to architects. Their status and use will now need to be revised to take into account the full potential of the conditions of interim prevalent in Bucharest. Areas and ways of negotiation will have to be invented that allow transgression to be harnessed in the definition of the modified, intensified blocks.

place/non-place

The zone of the Boulevard was a place before 1977. It became a non-place. What is at stake is its future.

> In the concrete reality of today's world, places and spaces, places and non-places intertwine and tangle together. The possibility of non-place is never absent from any place . . . Places and non-places are opposed (or attracted) like the words and notions that enable us to describe them . . . Words and images in transit through non-places can take root in the – still diverse – places where people still try to construct part of their daily life.[28]

Marc Augé's analysis associates words to spaces and political decisions to places, associations that bring us all the way to the beginning of this essay when the Dada poem also *Arc* connected words with lines.

a project in Bucharest interweaving tensions, collisions, conflicting programmes and different kinds of lines

In the Bucharest of 1995, a new project calls for other expectations and work methods. A good point of departure might be a kind of reversal of the process that took place between 1977 and 1989. Projects may start by enabling the current collisions behind the walls to engender conflicting programmes for an architecture of interweaving. The threads or lines may be of different kinds, colours and textures. As in a carpet, they may be knotted, combined, grown even, the overall pattern evolving from the given, almost chaotic situation. Fragmentary building and fragmentary programmes would begin to form an assemblage in its territoriality, aware of the passage through de-territorialisation, with a re-assessed content and given the expression of the work. The introduction of collage techniques that formed the Magheru Boulevard may once again prove fruitful.

use of collage

Such a project was prefigured by Tzara:

Dada is a state of mind. That is why it transforms itself according to races and events. Dada applies itself to everything, and yet it is nothing, it is the point where the yes and the no and all the opposites meet, not solemnly in the castles of human philosophies, but very simply at street corners, like dogs and grasshoppers.[29]

The array of methods proposed by Dada is describing the whole range of issues raised by the complex, by the momentary condition, the unfinished. Dada embraces the difficult situation that Bucharest may well exemplify.

contradiction

So, contradiction. All dadaists call upon it. Hugo Ball declares: 'The dadaist loves the extraordinary and even the absurd. He knows that life expresses itself in contradiction . . .'

Tzara proclaims that 'the true dadas are against DADA' and that '*order = disorder; me = non-me; affirmation = negation*' . . .

'interweaving of opposites and of all the contradictions' (Tzara)[30]

Better than an attempt at playback in reverse as a starting point, *contradiction* of the process that led to the Bucharest of today may be more fruitful. To apply this method to the House of the Parliament would require the removal of all decoration and fittings which could be sold. The building should then be re-planned starting from the existing and denuded structure. The constructional logic would remain, the programme would be reconsidered as presented above and the newly organised form would be witness to the incidence of the process. The undoubtedly well-crafted rich materials could then be integrated in projects and buildings chosen by the market (the success of the sale of the Berlin Wall gives confidence that there may be a substantial revenue as the outcome of such an operation). Furthermore, the breaking up of the monolithic image of the building can only open up the possibility of a genuine change or line of flight moving beyond the wall and outside the black hole, to connect with other lines and grow with them. [31]

walls . . .

The ambiguous nature of walls makes even more sense of the scenario described above:

Stupid illusion:
to surround oneself with walls
then suddenly to feel
so free[32]

Hope in a DADA project

It may only be of interest to present the zone in question from Bucharest as a Dada project in as much as it is intriguingly consistent with a cultural history where the tradition of Romanian architecture is intrinsically linked to the European avant-garde.[33] I would not wish to suggest a historical project; instead a fictional one that can *include* rather than exclude with the pleasure and power of the flight of imagination. A fiction where all is true.

. . . and holes and wells

The Romanian soul is used to tragedy. This is inevitable but it is always followed by hope. The construction of the wall or the shrine demands the sacrifice of the most beloved. The master builder, Manole, jumps from the roof to his death, as there is no escape from the justice of power. The construction of the wall holds in its destiny the black hole. And there, down below, there springs hope for the future.

And from near the sky,　　　There sprang up a well,
From the roof on high,　　　A fountain so tiny
Down he fell to die!　　　Of scant water, briny,
And, lo, where he fell　　　So gentle to hear,
　　　　　　　　　　　　Wet with many a tear![34]

Notes

1 In Romanian, an arc is a bow, an arch, and a geometric term referring to a segment of a circle. It is also the title of a poem attributed to Tristan Tzara, but supposedly written by Lenin in 1905. In the present essay, it is particularly apt as a title as it contains the weapon, geometry, architecture, the wall and a hole in its structure.

2 My transcription and translation of the beginning of the manuscript for the poem *Arc* published in the collection of poems *De nos oiseaux*, Paris, 1929. Taken from a photo-facsimile of the manuscript published in Dominique Noguez, 'LENINE dada', trans Bernard Laffont, 1989.

3 I use this name in reference to the Andrey Tarkovsky film *Stalker*. The Zone is the forbidden territory of despair where hope is sought at the risk of the trespasser. The Stalker is the guide through the Zone.

4 Mircea Dinescu, *Exile on a Peppercorn*, Forest Books, (London), 1985.

5 I refer to the thin section buildings that appear to have been designed to give a continuous stage-like wall effect to the endless axial boulevard. What happens behind is revealing: makeshift extensions gain one more precious metre of covered dwelling, surviving fragments of the demolished city occupy what might have been courtyards within the block structure. Thus, the linearity implied by the facade blocks is resisted by the inevitable structures of accommodation pushing from behind.

6 Slavoj Zizek, *Tarrying with the Negative: Kant, Hegel and the Critique of Ideology*, Duke University Press, (Durham, North Carolina) 1993, Introduction, p1.

7 Gilles Deleuze and Félix Guattari, *A Thousand Plateaux: capitalism and schizophrenia*, The Athlone Press, (London), 1988, pp167-68.

8 Ibid, p172.

9 Ibid, p172-73.

10 Attributed to Tristan Tzara, *Arc*, op cit, [author's annotation].

11 Maurice Blanchot, 'L'amitié', in *A Thousand Plateaux*, p227.

12 Gilles Deleuze and Félix Guattari, op cit, p228.

13 Ibid, p229.

14 In Herschel B Chipp, *Theories of Modern Art – a source book by artists and critics*, University of California Press, (Berkeley),1968, pp388-89.

15 In Dominique Noguez, 'LENINE dada', p116.

16 Gilles Deleuze and Félix Guattari, op cit, p215.

17 Gilles Deleuze and Félix Guattari, op cit, p229 and text for note 13.

18 Gilles Deleuze and Félix Guattari, op cit, p432.

19 L Machedon and F Machedon, 'Modern Architecture in Romania, 1920-1940', in *Bucharest in the 1920s-1940s Between Avant-garde and Modernism*, Simetria Publishing House, (Union of Romanian Architects, Bucharest), p79.

20 Herschel B Chipp, op cit.

21 L Machedon and F Machedon, op cit, p89, n10, quoted from 'Interiorul (the Interior)', in *Contimporanul* No 57-58, 1925, which Janco edited.

22 In *AA Files No 19*, pp56-68, The Architectural Association, (London), 1990.

23 Robin Evans, *Mies van der Rohe's Paradoxical Symmetries*, in *AA Files No 19*, p67 [author's italics].

24 In Dominique Noguez, 'LENINE dada' p96n, from *Lampisteries* preceded by *Seven Dada Manifestoes*.

25 Robin Evans, op cit, p67.

26 Ibid, p66.

27 Ibid, p67 [author's italics].

28 Marc Augé, *Non-places: introduction to an anthropology of supermodernity* Verso, (London), 1995, pp107-15.

29 In Herschel B Chipp, op cit, p389.

30 In Dominique Noguez, 'LENINE dada', pp99-100 [author's translation].

31 See text for note 16 and following paragraph.

32 M Dinescu, *Walls*, Forest Books, (London), 1985, p45.

33 See L and F Machedon, 'Modern Architecture in Romania', pp18-27, 69-91.

34 *Master Manole*, anon ballad, trans Dan Dutescu.

IOANA-MARIA SANDI
ETHICS FOR THE ARCHITECTURE OF ANOTHER EUROPE

I believe that architecture is ethics made visible in space.
Daniel Libeskind, July 1995.

Eastern European countries, like Romania, have an enormous potential for development, which is recognised and encouraged by the international community. In the presence or absence of theoretical debate, architecture will happen, regardless of whether one writes about it or not. The complexity of the contemporary condition, so strongly resisting assessment and diagnosis, imposes to a certain extent the attitude of letting the context act and speak for itself. Still, how can one understand this complexity? What 'kind' of complexity is it? And what approach is valid for an architect who actually works within these complex conditions?

An attempt to provide answers to such acute questions for architectural practice in Eastern Europe inevitably touches on the problems of exchange (cultural and economic) with Western countries and requires an adequate interpretation of the idea of European integration, to account for issues like difference and national identity. Within their local confines, the following comments – which relate almost entirely to the Romanian context – are intended to establish a moment of specificity which will hopefully pertain to more general aspects of European architecture, and will contribute to the birth of an open debate.

The complexity of an incomplete modernity
Stepan Mestrovici comprehensibly documents what he calls 'the confluence of post-modernism with post-Communism',[1] as two facets of the general failure of the Western Enlightenment project. Whether one subscribes to his terminology or not, knowing the contradictions inherent in the concept of post-modernity or other notions like late-modernity, post-capitalism, or even the on-going modern crisis, it can be said that they all attempt to cover common ground and to designate contemporary phenomena that cannot strictly be called modern. One way to understand the complexity of the Romanian (and Eastern European) context resides in the coincidence of the crisis of an over-achieved modernity in economically advanced Western countries, where the possibilities of fulfilment of the Enlightenment project are saturated, with the crisis of a yet incomplete project of modernity in the East – a coincidence which also reveals the contradictions of modernity as a cultural phenomenon.

To be more precise, the crisis of overachievement is supposed to designate the mutations suffered by the modern way of life in economically and technologically advanced countries (sometimes called 'post-capitalist societies'). The reality of simulation described by both Jean Baudrillard and Umberto Eco has offered a new scale to address phenomena that can be seen to differ fundamentally from the initial foundations of the Enlightenment project. Multiplicity of truths in indeterministic scientific discourses, as opposed to the true-false dichotomy of positivism, or the interference of ethical values with the essentially value-free scientific judgement, and finally, the virtual participation in the media or the Internet as parallel, actual realities that blur the distinction between fiction and fact – are all instances of this over-achieved modernity.

As if to illustrate the very concept of crisis of modernity, countries like Romania are suspended somewhere between modernity and tradition, with no clear possibility of resorting to either. Lacking both the foundations of industrialism and Cartesianism, the modernism manifest in Romania from the 19th century throughout the first half of the 20th century was supported by a largely agricultural population. In the absence of an individualism of the Protestant kind (Orthodox religion is fundamentally collective in spirit – a condition visible in the exoteric architecture of the church), whatever individual identity emerged during the modernist decades, it became the central target of destruction for the communist totalitarian ideology aimed at the levelling of all social differences and the redefinition of moral values. Parallel to this, one can see the emergence of an 'individualism for survival' as a response to the oppressive conditions that broke down the structure of the civic society. In contemporary Romania, international modernity manifests itself as 'high-tech informatization' and transactional operations, as well as an abundance of simulated media images that, in the absence of both a collective consciousness of a traditional type and of a clearly defined modern individualism, accumulate into what might be called a collective imagination.

Complete oppression may also result in liberating effects, and one could argue that, to a certain extent, the communist totalitarian ideological attack on 'reactionary' moral values has actually reinforced the resistance of the ethical structure of the society. As argued above, in Romania the general effect of ideological oppression was one of fragmentation, but in the same time the mutations suffered by the civic structure did not empty it of ethical content. In consequence, the sublimation of social consciousness into imaginary consciousness, with the images often equated with symbols of consumerist power, is parallel to a resurrection of moral judgement whose newly recovered standards are used as a measure for all social and cultural phenomena. Overachieved and incomplete modernity hence overlaps in both the actual reality of virtual phenomena and in the new relevance of the ethical, which is no longer confined to the ideological domain – resulting in the complex and difficult to rationalise contemporary conditions.

The specifity of another Europe
The difficulties in understanding the specificity of Eastern European countries within the larger context of Europe are a result of the complexity of their context. There is a common, if implicit, perception of these countries as slightly backward or uncivilised according to Western cultural criteria, with a possible explanation in the half-century of ideological oppression they have suffered. Related to the same criteria and the condition of incomplete modernity, a 'minor culture' complex is apparent in most Eastern European countries, dominating, at least in recent history, their self-image and placing them in a constant state of struggling to

prove their 'Westernness', in spite of obvious differences.

A way of reacting to conditions imposing such an inferiority complex is the issue of national identity, in spite of its perilous links with nationalist ideology. This link can be understood in different ways, and hopefully between the extreme explanations available, one can find an insight into the cultural identity of these countries. On one side, Mircea Eliade writes passionately:[2]

The historic mission of the peoples is not always haloed by the same glamour. There are nations whose role in history is so obvious that nobody has ever thought to question it. But there are also less happy nations . . . Ignored, or misunderstood at best, the life of these nations is more intense . . . These peoples do not know the respite, calmness and joy of *creating in time.* Incessantly attacked, they can only think while defending themselves . . . A frontier people, the Romanians were subject to the most terrible barbarian invasions during the period they formed as a people, only to have, once they had organised their State, to cope with another big Asiatic threat – the Turks – for centuries on end. Nowadays, the historians discover the tragedy of the Romanians and of the peoples living in Southeast Europe, who bled for five centuries in order to prevent the Islamic colossus from penetrating into the heart of Europe.

Referring to the same facts, Paul Hockenos makes a sweeping analysis of the resurrection of Fascism in Eastern Europe, describing the 'little nation complex' as a fundamental component of nationalist ideology:[3]

Integral to Eastern European nationalism past and present is the inferiority complex of the small, young and long-suffering nation. Whatever its impassioned spokesmen may profess, the history of modern national identity throughout most of Eastern Europe dates back only to the late-19th century, a reality that they tend to compensate for with myths that locate national traditions as far back as the imagination stretches. As those same spokesmen rightly argue, if selectively, the history of their people is usually a tragic one, marred by invasions, occupations, world wars, betrayals, and economic and natural catastrophes. Although the national cultures often boast a rich heritage of poetry, literature, and music, their achievements have gone relatively unrecognised on the world stage, particularly in comparison to those of the Western European nations . . . The very tone – humble, patient, self-pitying and misunderstood – is typical of almost all Eastern European nationalisms . . . The Romanians must therefore stand up for themselves, for their own culture, their own values and traditions, rather than allow some foreign power to dictate their destiny.

The first of these two extreme attitudes stems from the inter-war nationalist right-wing philosophical and political trends in Romanian culture. The second, however speaking from the tolerant point of view of Western liberal democracy, risks overlooking the specificity of the context under discussion, hence becoming anything but tolerant.

Both East and West live under the sign of the ideal of a united Europe, but this can be understood in various ways. One can take the view of a unifying strategy which involves the levelling of all differences in the favour of a homogenous community – and according to the standards set up by modern Western culture, countries like Romania remain irrevocably backward, unable to complete a modernity which is anyway in crisis and struggling to achieve a liberal democracy always slippery in the absence of a tradition of

The architecture of the city of Bucharest is European in many contrasting aspects, from 19th-century French Classicism (centre) to Oriental influences in the older traditional urban fabric (below). In the Lipscani area of central Bucharest many of the old buidings are decaying rapidly (above). In 1992 the British Know How Fund was approached by the Union of Romanian Architects to prepare a report on the improvement of the Lipscani district, an area containing markets and small businesses, the financial district and ruins of many historic buildings. PAGE 31: Steve Ibbotsen with Terry Farrell and Partners were commissioned to put forward strategic suggestions for a regeneration which would occur in stages and which could promote a positive domino effect. The basic ideas are helping to change attitudes and some of the early proposals, including the renovation of the 16th century Princely Palace, are now in place, and already signs of improvement are visible.

pre-capitalist social relations. Slavoj Zizek would go as far as to argue that the very identity of liberal democracy relies on an exclusion:

> The problem with the liberal democracy is that a priori, for structural reasons, it cannot be universalised . . . This split (between democracy and non-democracy) is therefore, *the very form of universality of the liberal democracy:* the liberal-democratic 'new world order' affirms its universal scope by way of imposing this split as the determining antagonism, the structuring principle, of inter- and international relations . . . the very *identity* of the liberal-democratic 'order' consist in the *scissure* which separates its 'inside' from its 'outside'.

Whether conscious or not, the pressure of Western standards results in Eastern Europe's (self-)perception as backward and unfortunate, a perception endorsed by the obvious material difficulties and the economic discrepancy between East and West. Without doubting for an instant the ideal of a united Europe, what should be called into question are the strategies of unification which impose the levelling of differences. There is a well known paradox in the fact that the availability of information leads not to uniformity but to differentiation and specificity, a result not of the choice available but of the actual choices made. It is possible that the attempts to rationalise according to Western (Enlightenment) standards cultures of multiple origins like those of Eastern Europe endorse the split described by Slavoj Zizek.

Alternatively, the exchange with Western Europe could be more of a bilateral operation, and the strategy of unification for a European Community could work as much towards expanding the notion of 'Europeanness' as towards imposing standards for the belonging to this category. For almost 50 years some of the European countries have lived in complete isolation – and their identity was forgotten as a result. This identity has now to be recognised in its complexity, fragmentation and contradictions as very much a European identity, and the criteria which were laid at the foundation of the notion of European union modified accordingly (the alternative would be to change the name of the European union into Western European union, would such mutations be found incompatible with a unifying strategy).

The quest for a valid architectural approach

Like other aspects of culture, the architecture of countries like Romania takes place between heroic attempts to import Western standards and their total negation. The specificity of a context in which religion is revived as a public value after 45 years of official denial; in which collective concerns are often sublimated into nationalism; where people tend to look abroad for models and those provided by frenetic consumerism become new collective symbols of power; in which daily life happens in the shadow of the explicit (built) or implicit (felt and acted) legacy of communist totalitarianism, translates into incredibly complex practical and philosophical constraints. However, the complex and difficult context does not necessarily equate with the lack of architectural value, and one should be aware of the inherent richness of such cultural conditions which can result in new ways of making buildings.

The architecture built in contemporary Romania echoes to a certain extent the architectural approaches devised by some international architects working within the complex conditions of 'post-capitalist' countries. Most of the categories of buildings are an operative response to the multiple constraints of the context. From a commercial point of view (the battle for a commission) or its related philosophical explanation (the equality of value be-

tween the architect's aspirations and the client's taste which can be seen to reflect more than anything else the specificity of the context), one architectural approach finds its justification in the complete subordination of architectural intention to client requirements. In its cynical pragmatism, this attitude touches on an ultra-rationalist quest for efficiency which at the same time denies the possibility of ethical judgement. However, the renunciation of moral (ideological) judgement by the architect is not followed by a renunciation of the same values in the case of the user or the critic, such that the architect can be criticised eventually for a lack of moral structure. Some of the architects who work with an operative approach of this kind in the Romanian context attempt to articulate an explanation for their work, recognising implicitly the ethical problems raised by such an approach.[4]

Another approach, documented in the architecture of Dorin Stefan, understands with enormous intelligence and insight the complexity of the context in all its limiting characteristics, while recognising that there are no apparent alternatives to an operative approach, that there are no ways of imposing personal or ideological aspirations on a reality which is not able to meet them. The ethical content of this architecture is more obvious as it painfully raises questions on the value of the outcome and consequently on the enabling or disabling potential of the Romanian order of complexity.

This specific complexity attaches some value to all architectural strategies, rejecting attempts to achieve an ideologically-free efficiency like the one exercised by Western architects in complex post-capitalist conditions. In a country where everything is judged in an attempt to recover a lost morality and civic structure, the kind of architecture which should get built is firstly an ethical and political issue before it becomes architectural.

In response to the initial uncertainty regarding the necessity of theoretical or philosophical articulation (while buildings get built in spite of its presence or absence), one can begin to outline an explanation which is grounded in the specificity of the Romanian context and the new relevance of ethical problems. In modern societies where collective consciousness has been replaced by subjective judgements and beliefs, the architect's only possible role is that of a mediator of the social context into an architectural social content. Trained for an extraordinary sensitivity, the architect's work can acquire a cathartic power to release and illuminate the understanding and the experiences of other people, to ultimately make 'ethics visible in space'. This mediation will never be value-free so long as the architect's role is an active one. In societies like Romania, where ethical judgement interferes with the measure of all phenomena, the architect is invested with the power to say what is right and what is wrong, even if this judgement falls within ideological discourses. The architect is situated ethically both as citizen and as professional, hence the architectural intention should be of a different value from the client's taste or the market requirements. In this sense, the architect is entitled to, and required to, create a vision in the sense of a reciprocity between reflection and praxis.

The difference between architectural approach and architectural vision is that which would enable the ethical dimension to be consciously accounted for in architecture. Architectural approaches can be insightful, intelligent and efficient *vis-à-vis* the complexity of the Romanian context, but they remain idiosyncratic as long as they rely on the strictly architectural means of expression. Because of the new ethical dimension emerging within the Eastern European societies, the architectural approach can and should be articulate, intelligible, communicable and debatable, such that it becomes part of a collective endeavour. A useful, though not exclusive way to enact such an architectural vision would be through the political attitude of a school.

To find suggestions on what form such an integration of praxis with reflection could find in contemporary Romania to account for both the specific complexity and the possibilities of exchange with the rest of Europe, one could follow the example of a recurring phenomenon in Romanian culture known as *Romanian synthesis* after the concept formulated by the historian Nicolae Iorga. In several remarkable instances, the architecture of Romania has adopted a synthesis of foreign (French, Oriental, Italian or German) influences which have been adapted to suit the local needs by means of mutations within the vernacular.

Bearing in mind the complex specificity of the context, another justification for the search for a vision is that none of the available foreign models seems to fit Romanian contemporary society. Between moral problems of how buildings can be built and material problems of what can be built, between modernity and tradition, one could argue that a resolution of the identity crisis could be found in a reassessment of the vernacular, in the continuous tradition of the Romanian synthesis.

In Zizek's words, the only way to understand the complementarity of modernity and tradition lies in the irreversibility of the modern project: 'any true return to tradition is a priori impossible, its role is simply to serve as a shock-absorber for the process of modernisation.' As in previous instances of Romanian synthesis, the vernacular can offer the core on which international models can be grafted and accommodated. The exchange with Western standards would therefore be twofold: the inability of coping with Western technological standards requires a different philosophy, of which vernacular is one of the possibilities; at the same time, Eastern countries would still rely on the input of Western expertise, precisely because of the discrepancy in technological standards. The work of Imre Makovecz in the neighbouring country of Hungary is an excellent example on how one could develop an appropriate technology within the vernacular tradition, and also strike the chord of the forgotten collective consciousness. Finally, the reinterpretation of the vernacular should not be seen as the quest for a style, and should aim for deeper forms of continuity in the architectural identity of the country. It is not in the formal outlook of the tradition but in its content, in its *way of living and operating* that one could find a core to support the complex requirements of the contemporary context and the necessary exchanges with the rest of Europe.

Although there are very few people who would openly deny moral competence, there is a different value given to accepting the responsibility of political action on a public level which could begin to restore a civic structure to societies as confused as those of the post-communist countries. Like everything in Eastern Europe, architecture is today in a state of *quo vadis?* The architecture of the other Europe can either go forwards, or go backwards. Or perhaps it could go elsewhere?

Notes

1 Stepan Mestrovici, *The Balkanization of the West*, Routledge, (London), 1994.
2 Mircea Eliade, *The Romanians: A Concise History*, Roza Vinturilor, (Bucharest), 1992.
3 Paul Hockenos, *Free to Hate*, Routledge, (London), 1993.
4 Ioan Andreescu's lecture at the 'Beyond the Wall' conference in Bucharest, July 1995.

The report put forward: FROM ABOVE: Improvements to shop fronts and the removal of the market stalls on Lipscani Street; pedestrianisation where possible, repaving of road surfaces and new street furniture; increased use of open space around buildings, including public use of courtyards, replanting and increased accessiblity

DORIN STEFAN
X-RAYING OF A SPATIAL BLINK

I sense somehow that space gets tired. In those moments of tiredness, when the 'space eyelids' are heavy, it is the time of architecture.

The architecture could be the 'prop' holding the 'space eyelids' open, similar to Salvador Dali's props sustaining the melting of space. Through these eyelids, the architects are pouring new forms; liquid crystal which will provide the space with 'a new look'. A new look for a space which is tired. A new look could be obsessive, grand and decadent.

In between space and architecture there is the 'interface' of reality. The reality everyone is defining, however they are able, is self-defining from the context.

In the West, the architecture is stronger than the reality. At the border between West and East, the reality is stronger than the architecture – it converts the spirit too. When the space is tired, 'well prepared' men, with 'props', are watching for the weak moment to prop it up with architectural 'wedges' – spatial 'wedges' which uphold the spirit. When the 'space' is blinking the architects are erecting the Wall. The architecture is the 'sliver' in the eye of the blinking space. 'Slivers' chopped from reality. When the architecture is weaker than the reality those slivers remain simple supports. They cannot sustain the spirit enough, unlike the architecture which 'surrounds' the reality. Can we save the architecture when reality is stronger?

Tired of undistilled form and the misunderstood ornament, the Romanian space is sleeping. Are we going to wake it or let it sleep? I feel that at this time the reality is obliging me not to invent, but to heal, to cover, to wrap, to lay wings over a tired space. The Western reality distilled itself continuously: in the East time was permanently cut short. This led to lost potential. The Romanian reality was,

and is, one of co-existence; our time and space neighbours the Western one. The co-existence started in the 19th century, and the synchronisation to the Western pulse reached perfection through the 1920s and 30s. After 1945 the phasing out started, although an organic cohesion was always present. Organic cohesion means that one cannot neighbour anyone who is dissimilar. In the East/West situation one of the neighbours is moving away or is looking for a different cohesion. For these reasons we 'wrap' whatever someone else has produced – usually Western architecture. Working with this 'wrapped' architecture hoping to rediscover a certainty (and I do not mean a new 'form follows function').

In 1990 my office and our clients were fascinated with the grand architectural programmes which were supposed to occupy the multitude of empty spaces left by Ceausescu's 'planning schemes'. But the euphoric state faded away as quickly: the foundations were abandoned. Our interest was diverted toward apparently cheaper projects: used spaces, living ruins or concrete skeletons.

Bioprod Services and Leisure Centre, shown here, effectively started off revamping, or dressing-up semi-industrial spaces located in a park on a lake shore in Bucharest. In the end, an office tower was erected over a large water tank.

Other projects have involved the different forms of wrapping, covering or moulding, folding and forming. A proposal for Ceausescu's 'Palace for the People' would cover it with a lndscaped earth mass.

Parallel to the 'shell effect', soft details are applied which do not require high technology. Articulated details become cast details: the materials 'planting' into one another.

Why? Perhaps . . . the space is tired.

Perspective of the office tower, Bioprod Services and Leisure Centre

*Bioprod Services and Leisure Centre, site axonometric
and aerial view of computer-generated model*

MIROSLAV MASAK
SIX YEARS AFTER THE VELVET REVOLUTION

Our convalescence from the difficult past has already lasted six years, a convalescence from an illness which was effected by a long isolation, and gave rise to a life lived under a different value system. Recovery progresses slowly, all important aspects of life having been affected: morality, education, dexterity, and prosperity. We are marked by scepticism, by an unwillingness to accept personal responsibility, and an inclination to 'pass the buck'. Today the driving force is money, and our society feels that in the current situation is to be found a perfunctory start towards its enrichment. We should be young, healthy, beautiful and rich. In six years, our inner life has changed. The world has stopped perceiving us as a nice, post-totalitarian curiosity, it has begun to see us as a partner, as a civilised country whose institutions, businesses and individuals must independently make their way in a competitive world.

Prague, and our other cities, are awash with guests from around the world. Thousands of young Americans believe that it is possible to draw energy from these cities. God bless them. Returning the countryside and cities to their former dignity, dynamism and beauty will be a difficult task, as long as the cities are represented by an inexperienced post-November civic government and by the interests of new entrepreneurs. To anticipate civic interest in a cultured renewal of the country's heritage, and in the finer questions of architectonic creation, would be premature.

Our building activity has shifted from the city's periphery to more attractive locales. The composition of this activity has shifted too, where once dominated by the construction of social housing, this has been supplanted by an excess of banks, commercial buildings and rental offices. Most of the large state building companies have collapsed, though the smaller private firms are proving more resilient. With the broadening of technological and material possibilities, the quality of construction is improving. Architects, who for the last 40 years were employed by state, regional or large resort project institutes, are adjusting daily to work as independent business people. The November transition promptly knocked a hole in our professional isolation. It enabled us once again to perceive all manner of European architecture. More slowly, however, we are redeveloping our sense of high standards, our feeling for building detail, our need to learn through experience, to find our self-confidence and faith in the ability to go one's own way.

Among architectural projects from the post-November period you will find examples of renewed links to Czech Functionalism, but also to the Wagner school of the turn of the century; you will find accents of Contextualism, of Czech High-Tech, Deconstructivism and New Simplicity. The same broad plurality of conceptions that you can find in other European countries. The awarded projects of our architectural 'Grand Prix' were examples of Post-Modernism: Theatre on a String in Brno by Vaclav Kralicek; High-Tech: a multi-purpose stage spiral in Prague by Kulik, Louda, Smetana and Styblo; Contextualism: a sewage plant on the river Upa by Roman Koucky; and New Modern or New Simplicity: a speculative office building in Prague by ADNS Studio. Plurality is represented, but not in ostentatious gestures. We do not live, until now, under conditions which would provoke us to artistic speculation, to exhibitions of rather complicated forms and technologies. The characteristic features of our recent architecture are sobriety, materiality, and austerity which harmonise with, and which, in a certain way, are kindred with our national mentality. These manifest primarily in the work of the younger generation from Brno, Liberec, Ceske Budejovice and Prague. Stimulated by the remarkable heritage of the 20s and 30s, these examples of contemporary Czech projects help to establish a new, high standard of architecture.

The year 2000 is just around the corner and the power of social and artistic vision has evaporated. Again the question arises: do we leave things as they are and only enter into dialogue with those issues we engage, or do we attempt to actively define a new order and style? Being aware of the fact that our civilisation is the first in history to embrace the entire globe, propelling us towards a common destiny, we should answer this question. But I am afraid we have not recovered enough yet to define any reasonable answer to a global question of a potentiality, necessity, and acceptability of any order and style.

OPPOSITE: Martin Krupauer, Jiri Stritecky and Atelier 8000, commercial bank in Ceske Budejovice, 1992-94

BENJAMIN FRAGNER
DIFFERENT YET AGAIN

It is not easy to really get a feeling for space in central Europe, neither in order to encourage discussion nor when the aim is a more fundamental one related to the normal life of every day. It is no surprise that such matters soon lose their relevance. In the Czech Lands and in Prague, in particular, the typical facades and *mélange* of styles are not just a result of interweaving different cultures and approaches to creation. Looking backwards we can see that this mixture also grew out of very pragmatic economic aims, personal tastes and, in certain periods of history, of unsustainable ideologies.

If we wish to get a full picture of recent developments, it is worth starting with a series of events and exhibitions in the late 1980s.[1] There a certain resignation from the shadow of totalitarianism and intolerance of the official architectural values of that time was very clearly expressed. Some of the work exhibited took a somewhat ironic view of the current state of the art, while freer architectural works pointed out the need for changes in the system and offered suggestions as to how the industrial constructions of the devastated cityscapes could be brought to life.

Michal Brix's designs for the music pavilion at Mariánské Lázne were one of the projects that emerged from the debates at the turn of the decade. They were greeted both as pure art and as a direct reaction to decades of decline in building culture. His attempts to resurrect abandoned values were ignored by a regime for which both its form and style were ideologically unacceptable.

However the mere disappearance of political taboos did not suffice for the fulfilment of intellectual visions. There was still the quandary of the thousands of housing estates with their blocks of prefabricated panels, which serve as a constant reminder of aggressive totalitarian planning and of the deterioration of construction skills. Five years on they are a reminder of a past which may be gone but which still obscures our view. The irony is that flats in these condemned panel blocks are rising in value from day to day, while the construction of new flats stagnates.

Jan and Martin Sedlák have made a valuable contribution to solving the problems of the largest Prague housing estates, bringing

rational order to chaos and offering space for the plans of individual investors. The risks and conflicts of the current development are however legend and Prague is considering the strategy for its development. One contribution to this was the study 'Prague 2010' prepared for Prague city council by a multi-disciplinary group of experts in collaboration with the Eco Terra foundation.[2] It considered methods of reworking hitherto disregarded plans for the development of the capital city and included a contribution from the British Know How Fund, represented by the London-based firm Llewelyn & Davies.

The starting point of the new attempt to revive Czech architecture is therefore somewhat different from that which seemed so important back in 1989. After decades when politics were paramount, economic and property issues have come to the fore. The restitution laws returned buildings to their original owners and privatised state property or rented municipal land and buildings became prime commercial items overnight. Now architects are up against concrete legal owners rather than the weight of anonymous ideology which they were used to. For Western planners this situation may seem banal but it has brought a whole new range of problems for professionals here, from the fierce competition for commissions to the need to satisfy investors' demands, which could well be in conflict with professional ethics or the public interest, with common taste or the preservation of the common architectural heritage.

The gradual remodelling of Prague is a clear demonstration of those features typical of the post-revolutionising scene in the Czech Republic. As yet there have been few major issues such as the plans for the new international airport by the Brix-Franta studio. Apart from shop interiors, luxury offices and restaurants, the most common architectural projects are those for open spaces in the cityscape – mostly courtyards and passages, reconstruction of old and often historically important buildings, and extensions to existing buildings. This is comparable to the period between the wars, when Prague was adorned with many noteworthy modern buildings.

This may be one reason why Czech architecture is re-evaluating the values of early modern architecture, its view of life and morality. For

OPPOSITE: Interior of the Theatre Spiral, Prague, 1992, by Tomas Kulik, Jan Louda, Jindrich Smetana and Zbysek Styblo

Speculative office building in Prague, by ADNS Studio – Václav Alda, Petr Dvorák, Martin Nemec and Ján Stempel

many architects today they symbolise a return to democracy. The formal austerity of rationalist functionalism has inspired the work of the ADNS Studio (Václav Alda, Petr Dvorák, Martin Nemec, Jan Stempel).

The demand that architecture reflect the economic success of those commissioning it is a sign of the times. The work of the OMICRON-K Studio bears a very modern mark of ambition (International Business Centre on Tesnov and Pexider office block on Vinohrady, Prague), as does the new office block on the Myslbek site of the central Na príkope street. Constructed to the plans of an association of Czech and French architects (Zdenek Hölzel, Jan Kerel and Claude Parent), it is taking shape on what is probably the most valuable site in the central city district.

Another of the best known buildings in Prague today is that on a demolition site on the Rasínovo Embankment. Designed by American Frank Gehry and the Czech architect Vlado Milunic, it has aroused fervent praise and condemnation on the part of the public. It is noteworthy as the first occasion since 1989 that a noted Western architect has collaborated on a building in Prague, and also for the interest it has aroused in the general public on the question of new buildings.

The current building boom also poses problems from the point of view of architecture. Those involved in planning reconstructions, modernisations, extensions and courtyard constructions have an unrepeatable opportu- nity to bring together modern ideas and history, confronting styles and combining modern and traditional materials, and bringing together different forms. (This is very clear in the plans of Petr Kordovsky, the Safer-Hájek studio and, in a different mode, by Atelíer 8000.) At the same time, their architecture is a Trojan horse, moving into hidden, often ignored but always intimate sites in the city.

There is a growing debate as to what cultural and social limitations are needed. Most new buildings are justified by the argument that the city must not be allowed to become a museum or an archive of dead memories, a petrified historical document, as this would mean the destruction of what is first and foremost a human habitation. Such arguments also recall the philosophical argument for responsibility in urban development presented by Jacques Derrida at the conference 'Prague – the Future of a Historic City', in 1991.[3]

Some years on from that, the situation is different yet again and Derrida's words have become still more poignant. While the architecture of the newly completed buildings is bringing new life into the environment in formal, visual terms, it is almost purely limited to office blocks and offices which are emptied of their tenants in the evening or, in the centre, to the hotels and shops catering for the tourists and business travellers passing through the city. Paradoxically this very ambition is helping to put an end to the natural life of the city.
Translated by April Retter

Notes

1 The first exhibition was organised in 1985 under the title of *Malovaná architektura (Painted Architecture)* by a scientific and technical journal *Technicky magazin*. It was followed by other exhibitions *Urbanita 86, 88* to 90, which were concerned less with questions of style than with the devastation of Czech towns and countryside and with the failings of professional ethics of architects and town planners. Most of the more interesting architects, young and not so young, were involved, including those whose work is mentioned here. See 'Urbanita: Komunikace na pomezí' in *Ceská architektura 1945 az 1995*, the Society of Czech Architects, (Prague), 1995.

2 Bohuslav Blazek, 'Praha 2010, Problems of Prague', part 1, supplement to *T94-Technicky magazín*, June 1994. *See also* Jan Kasl, Milan Turba, Bohuslav Blazek, Benjamin Fragner, 'Praha 2010, City at the crossroads', part 2, supplement to *T94-Technicky magazín*, November 1994.

3 Jacques Derrida, 'Generations d'une ville: mémoire, prophétie, responsabilités' in *Prague - Avenir d'une ville historique capitale* (Czech edition *Praha. Budoucnost historického mesta)* , Editions de l'Aube, Association pour la communauté culturelle européenne, (Paris), 1992.

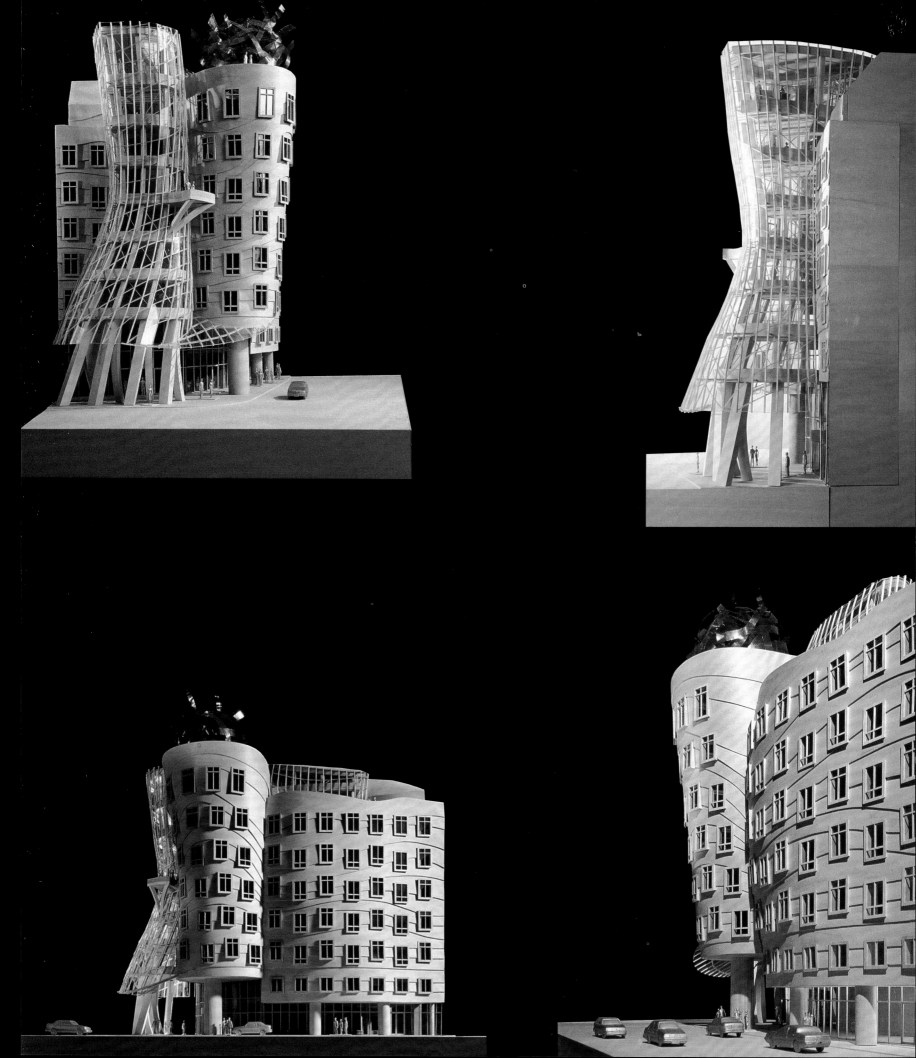

FRANK GEHRY

NATIONALE-NEDERLANDEN OFFICE BUILDING
Prague

Located along the Vltava river front within walking distance of the National Theatre and other prominent cultural facilities, the site is one of only three in the historic district of Prague where new construction is being permitted. The previous building on the site was destroyed accidentally by an American bomber during World War II. The corner site's adjacency to an unusually shaped public square calls for a twin tower scheme that makes a smooth transition from street to street, while at the same time creating a strong visual focus. This massing strategy also establishes a sculptural dialogue appropriate to its urban context.

On the ground level, directly accessible from the river front and public square, is a cafe and 200 square metres of retail space. Offices occupy five floors and are designed to fulfil the most rigorous requirements of the client. The spaces directly behind the twin towers are to be used as special offices or conference rooms. Finally, a bar and restaurant occupy the top level of the building to take full advantage of the spectacular view of the Prague skyline which includes views of the castle.

The main exterior facade, overlooking the river bank, responds to the rich textures and scale of the adjacent row houses. Its staggered windows and horizontal striations gradually break into a wave pattern that relates to the undulating cornice lines of the lively neighbouring river front facades. It will be constructed of precast concrete panels with a plaster finish which is common to the local Prague architecture.

The twin towers: one developed as a cylindrical solid volume, the other a tapering glass tower, are supported by a number of sculptural columns, creating a small covered entrance plaza for the offices above. Furthermore, the glass tower will be comprised of two layers of steel-supported glass curtain wall. The interior layer is the actual wall of the building with the sculptural outer layer

acting as a screen for the office spaces underneath.

For this project, three-dimensional computer modelling played a key role in supplementing the traditional methods of documentation, bidding, and quality control. This approach to three-dimensional computer modelling has been developed to link the design process more closely to fabrication and construction technologies as opposed to the imaging software more typically used by architects. The approach is intended to support and expand on a design process which relies heavily on building physical architectural study models and mock-ups.

Frank Gehry worked with Vlado Milunic, the first collaboration of a Western architect with an architect from the Czech Republic, to produce this design which is presently under construction.

Typical office floor plan

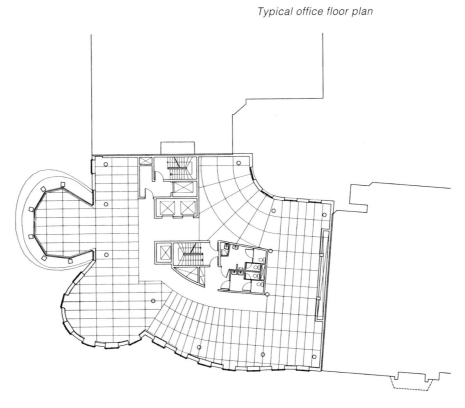

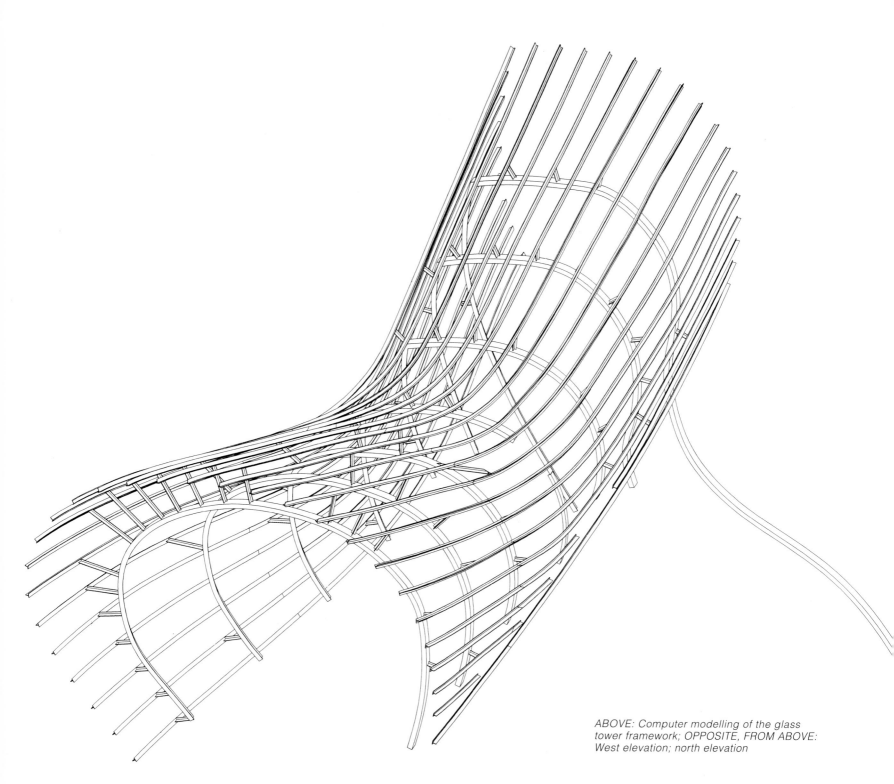

ABOVE: Computer modelling of the glass tower framework; OPPOSITE, FROM ABOVE: West elevation; north elevation

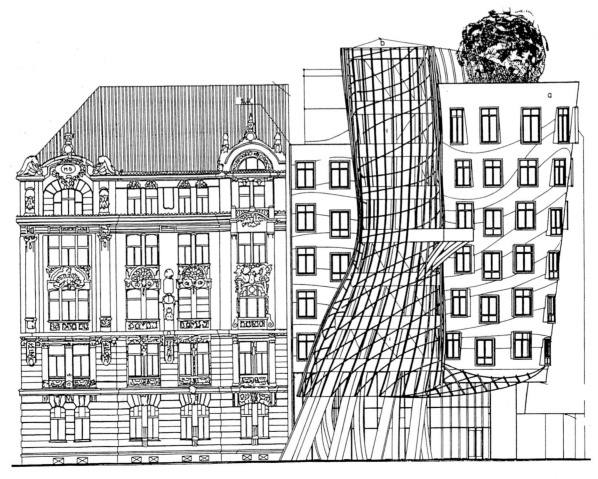

ROMAN KOUCKY
LABE PUBLISHING HOUSE
Usti nad Labam

This publishing house, which won the Czech Republic's *Grand Prix* for small architecture and design in architecture, attempts to elevate common materials by non-traditional usage and quality crafts-manship. Against a background of terrazzo tiles, white emulsion paint and smooth plaster, materials such as water-proof plywood, raw iron, leather and glass are applied in details, their natural colour and surface unadorned and structurally honest.

The clients required the conservation of the original building, a tenant house built in 1906, without altering its New Gothic shell, while converting it for use as the offices of a regional newspaper. The addition of visual links, bright surfaces and new internal elements has opened up the small rooms.

From the entrance hall an uplit glass and terrazzo counter extends through to the buffet bar to one side and the adver-tising department to the other, forming a barrier between the public and private space. The insertion of a central elevator behind the entrance desk enabled the bearing walls to be strengthened, rein-forcing the existing structure. In the meeting room located above the entrance hall, the carpet, designed by Zuzana Krajicovicova, has been mirrored in relief on the stucco ceiling.

Lighting is highly detailed, and supple-ments the jewel-like quality of the interior elements, with lines, spots and dispersed lighting effecting a playful game of light, shadow, and colour throughout.

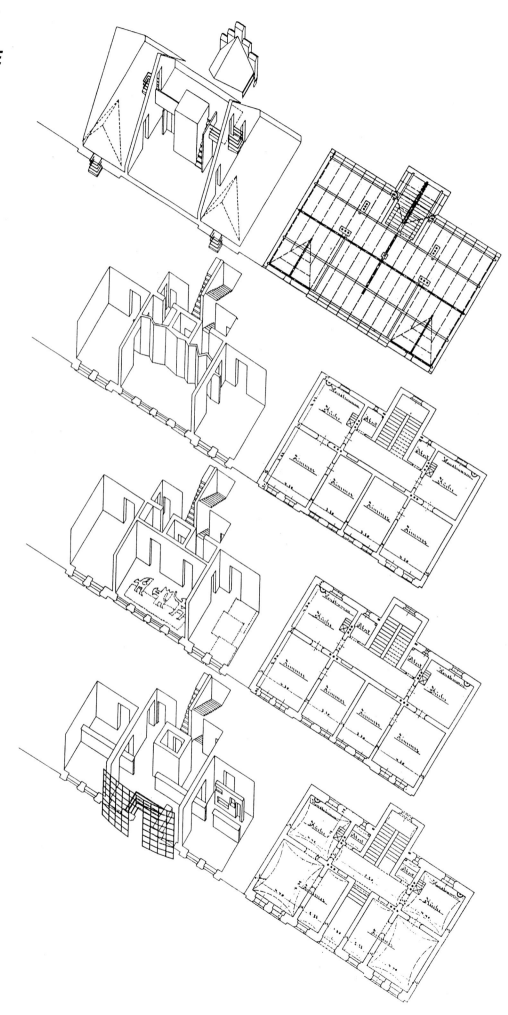

Axonometric showing the three-dimensional development of the scheme, transposed with the original plans of the building

SIAL
HYPOBANKA
Prague

The decision to place a new bank on the Square of the Republic once again raised a heated debate in the Czech press. Rather an intersection of several streets than a carefully defined urban space, the square has been the subject of several architectural competitions in the past. The site is among the last few spots in the centre still left open either for future civic use or for a commercial development.

Radim Kousal and the SIAL team won this competition in 1995. The practice consists of six partners: Otakar Binar, Karel Hubácek, Radim Kousal, Karel Novotny, Jirí Suchomel, Jaromir Syrovátko and 11 associates, with a further eight employees. Founded by architect Karel Hubácek in 1968, SIAL Architects & Engineers was forced to merge with the state owned Stavoprojekt system only three years later. The group survived and succeeded in maintaining its own profile of work for the next two decades. The office regained independence after the political turnover in 1990 and was privatised in 1991 as SIAL Architects and Engineers.

OPPOSITE: Elevation; worm's eye view perspective; FROM ABOVE: Site perspective; longitudinal section; ground floor plan

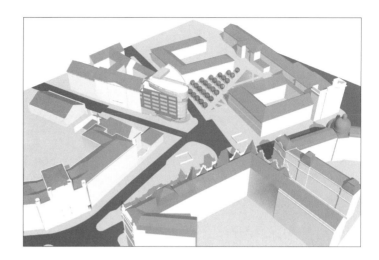

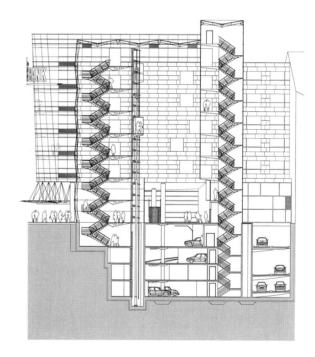

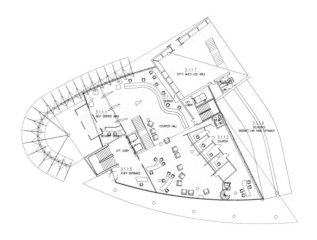

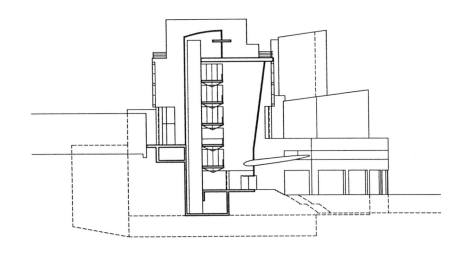

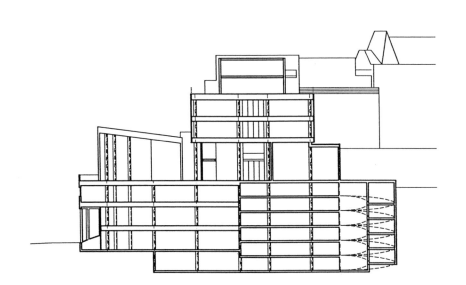

SYNER PALACE
Liberec

This mixed-use development study for Liberec contains retail, office, housing and parking facilities. It is on an empty corner site in the central area of Liberec.

The shape and massing of the building relects an interaction of two different urban scales and it utilises the given topographical features, sitting on the street edge. The central entrance hall with its elevator serves the rentable office floors and the residential village at the top of the building.

The architects for the scheme were Jirí Suchomel with Matthew Hardcastle, Niall McBrierty and Martin Saml.

OPPOSITE: Elevation; section;
ABOVE: Second floor plan; ground floor plan;
BELOW: Model

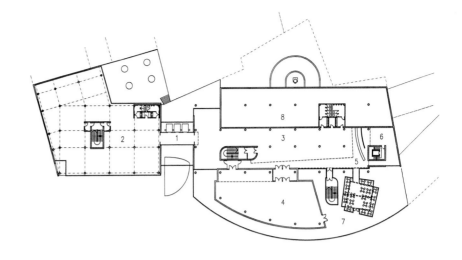

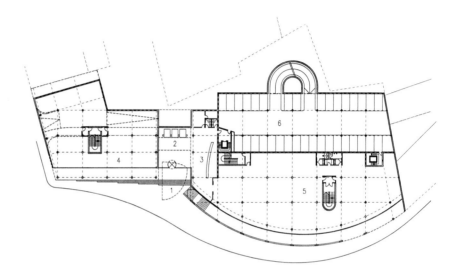

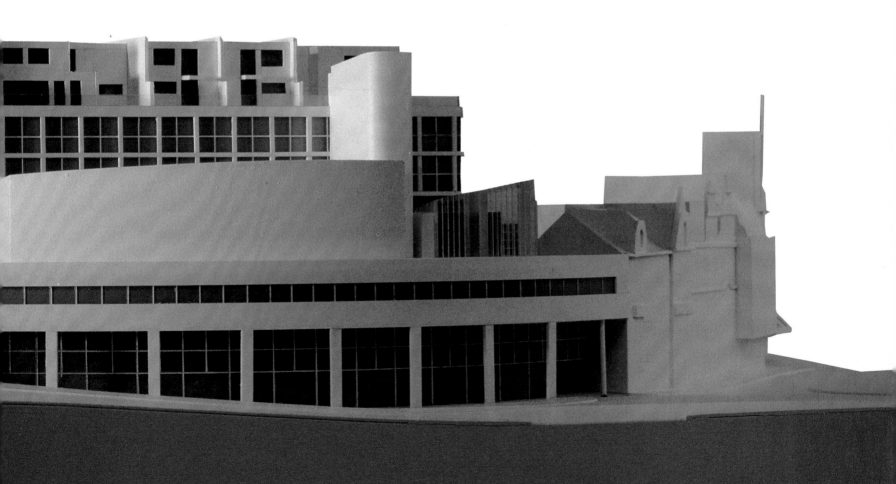

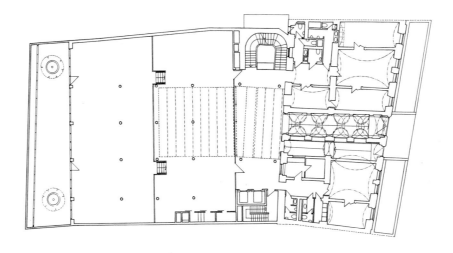

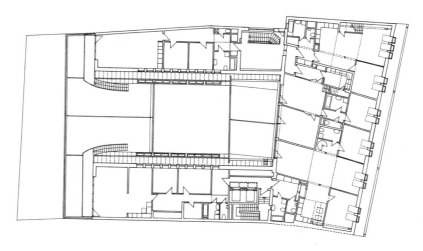

DA STUDIO
KRAKOVSKÁ STREET
Prague

DA Studio was formed in 1986 as an independent group, unusual for a time when most architects were part of the totalitarian State design institutes. They have slowly built up a practice based on pragmatic simplicity.

The Krakovská Street project is an attempt at joining a classical old house with a new building, creating a harmonious whole which becomes a dialogue between the two different parts.

In the inner city of Prague, 19th-century houses are generally preserved intact, with modern interventions hidden within the internal courtyards. The building in Krakovská Street is faced by the gables of the neighbouring houses, and only one side is open to the inside of the block.

The concept of the house works like a classical drama, comprising three distinct parts: the reconstructed old house, the modern house and a communication hall. The hall, a central atrium, forms the interface of the house where the two disparate sections meet. A glazed wall, the full height of the atrium, forms a visual link between the old semi-circular stair at one side and new vertical circulation on the other. The different levels are compensated by small bridges which replace the original galleries.

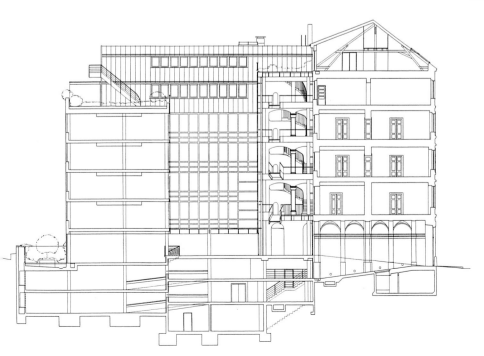

OPPOSITE, FROM ABOVE: First floor plan; views of model; typical floor plan; ABOVE: Rear view of model; section through the old and new buildings

JOSEF ONDRIAS AND JURAJ ZÁVODNY
VILLA IN BRATISLAVA
Slovakia

Modern architecture has served as a model towards which architecture always returns because it is such a source of steadiness. Returns to Modernism were more frequent in Slovakia than elsewhere and include major comebacks after World War II, after the period of Stalinism, during the 1950s, 60s and finally, 80s. These were impressive because of various forms of strong anti-Modernist opinions that can be found everywhere; from a basic political direction to consequent artistic classifications. The renewed Modernism is understood within its wider context and Jozef Ondrias and Juraj Závodny could easily join this stream.

The project for a villa in Bratislava, on the slope of a hill, had been inspired by the architecture of the 1920s and 30s; in its forms of construction, technological quality and architectural spirit.

The villa is an integrated unit, combining architectural concepts with perfect details. The form and position of the house was determined by the character of the land, and despite the fact that the lot for the villa was only 400 square metres, the design is free and grandiose.

The two-wing construction consists of two slightly shifted parts, both linked by a one-arm staircase which is bowed into a slight arch. The house is two-storeys at street level. stepping down to four storeys at the garden level.

When compared to other modern concepts, the villa bears similarities to Rietveld's Schröder house in Utrecht. Similar features include folding glass planes and internal separating walls. The verticality and use of the double chimney are similar to the new Douglas house by Richard Meier, in Harbor Springs.

Finally, the colour tones are slightly decadent, dominated by blue and pink, a combination which this team of architects frequently employs.

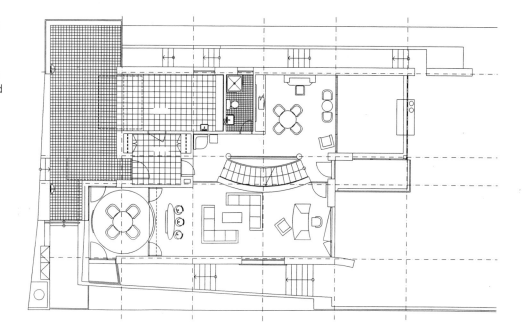

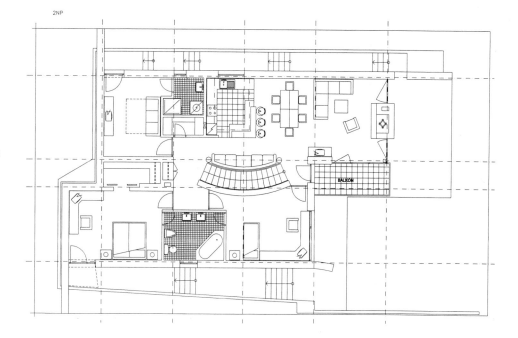

FROM ABOVE: Plan of the third floor; plan of the second floor

MYTNIK OFFICE BUILDING
Bratislava

The architects restored an inconspicuous town house with a balcony courtyard built in the 1930s. The building was renewed carefully, paying respect to the original design. The architects have covered the courtyard and created office space for a new bank. The architects' ambitions, however, went beyond ordinary house restoration: manifest in their novel use of fine arts.

The restored building proves that a connection between sculpture and architecture is not an obsolete concept. Similar to the multi-layered architectural approach, the architects were looking for a more profound story to be communicated through sculpture: a group of sculptures by Juraj Cutek and Rastislav Trizma, based on Greek mythology and the legend of Perseus, overlooks the central space.

Slovakian cultural heritage bears similarities to the situation of other small countries in peripheral parts of Europe. Here, on the edge of Eastern Europe, cultural expression is significantly affected by a nation's fight for its European status, and by a permanent realisation of the difference. The most important role is, however, played by a never-ending consciousness of its own cultural imperfection.

If we do not focus solely on the masterpieces, a number of tiny, but remarkable, cultural performances and architectural works can be found that draw our attention by their simplicity combined with an overall humanistic philosophy. This restored office building represents this new artistic and architectural creativity.

Matus Dulla and Henrieta Moravcikova

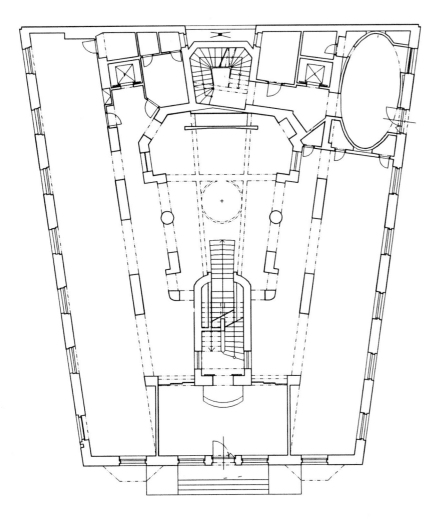

ABOVE: Plan of the ground floor; BELOW RIGHT: Before reconstruction

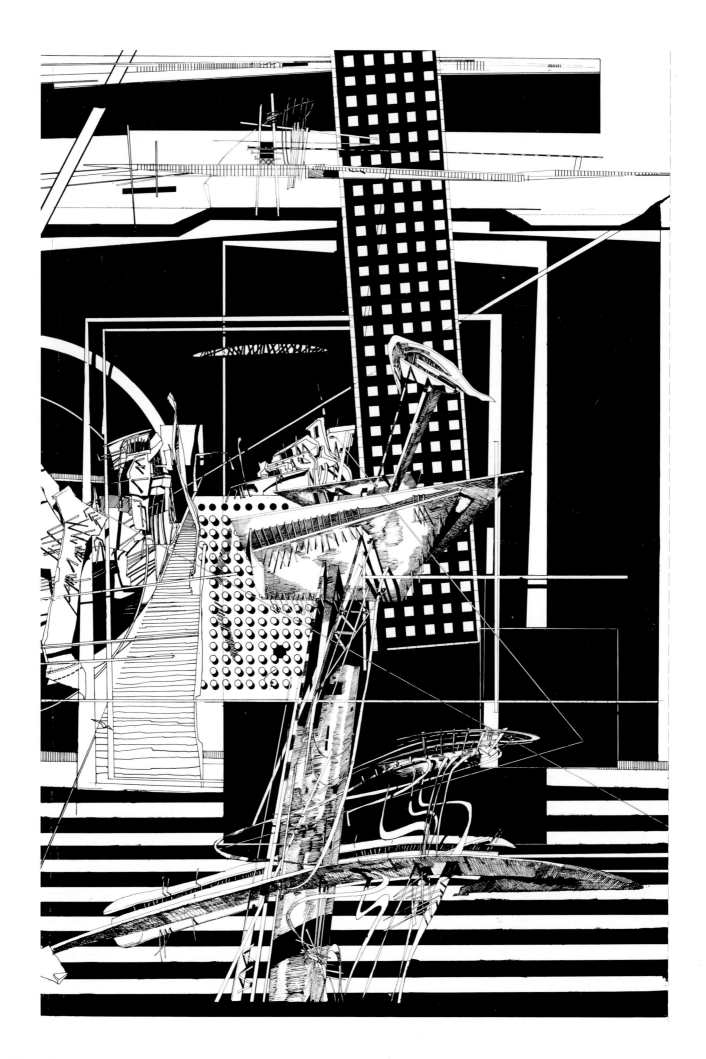

60 Slovakia

SPILLER FARMER
THE BRATISLAVA EXPERIENCE

The Spiller Farmer office in Bratislava, Slovakia was established in September 1991. The political and social context found then and the present conditions are very different. The UK has been particularly slow to recognise the possibilities of trading in Eastern Europe but this is starting to change as the economies strengthen. Property prices continue to rise particularly in the housing sector until, at this point, they approximately equal UK prices.

Bratislava, made capital after the negotiated breakup of old Czechoslovakia, has a rich and important history and this is reflected in the architecture of the historic centre; with its Eastern European Baroque and a skyline dominated by Hrad, the medieval castle. During the Communist era the city drastically expanded as a centre of primary industry, when the strategic advantages of its location, just across the Danube from Vienna and 130 kilometres from Budapest were recognised. This rapid expansion was manifested in the provision of a huge precast concrete panelled housing district called Petrazalka. The area currently houses one third of Bratislava's half a million inhabitants in 1200 towers.

The historic centre has always been the main target for foreign investors and much of our work is located in this area. Working in Bratislava has many advantages and disadvantages. One advantage is a lack of the stigma that young practices experience in other areas of Europe, especially in the UK. Another advantage is that because imported building elements such as door handles, lighting fittings and hand rail systems prove to be expensive, and time consuming to procure, various creative solutions to a variety of prosaic building issues allow an architectural concept to be followed deeply into the design without huge cost implications for the client. Disadvantages include little or no internal investment, virtually all real estate investors are foreign, and architects must take on a plethora of other roles to ensure the architectural commission in the long run. The juggling of financial packages, acquisition of sites and strategic and protocol advice (such as dealing with internal banking structures) normally outside the traditional architects' role, are time-consuming activities and inevitably involve some sort of equity stake in many larger projects. The office in Bratislava continues to grow, as it has over the last four years. The symbiosis between Bratislava and London has resulted in some very interesting projects and approaches that would not have been entertained in our native UK. Our experiences in Eastern Europe are crucial to the ongoing development of both the practice's commercial and theoretical work.
Laurie Farmer, Bratislava Office

OPPOSITE: Piestany Art Wall;
BELOW: Fountain

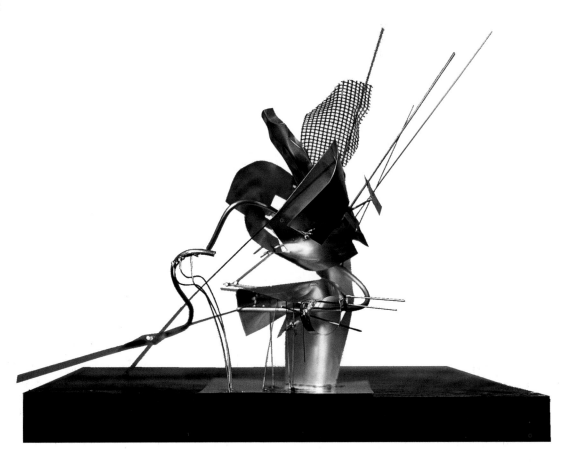

PENTHOUSE FLATS
Ruzinov, Bratislava, Slovakia

As the market economy takes effect in Bratislava, there is an emergent need for larger, more comfortable accommodation. This new housing should express an identity different from the ubiquitous precast concrete tower and slab blocks. The majority of the Bratislavan population lives in the depressing homogeneity of this particular type of housing form.

This project has three aims, which are to identify opportunities for further accommodation, develop strategies to improve the atmosphere of this particular development zone and to provide a much needed marker in this sea of ubiquity.

It immediately became obvious that the 'fifth elevation' (the roof) had the most potential for adaption and addition. The existing blocks are seven storeys high, structurally sound but architecturally poor.

A series of propositions was made that allowed the project to, be 'fast track' and be constructed at relatively low cost at little inconvenience to the existing tenants.

The drawings are not a final solution and are sufficiently flexible to allow the development to be variable in its design. The construction of the project is intended to be of steel and timber with large areas of glazing. The project will utilise local gypsy labour whose skills are in metal working. It is important that the flats are outward looking and the dynamic of being high above the ground is appreciated.

The new structure sits on its host, interfering with it minimally; the largest component of interference being the removal of the final stairwell window to facilitate a spectacular access to the penthouses, as the stair cants outside the envelope of the building before returning to the roof level.

To complete the project the common parts of the block will be refurbished and the surrounding landscape will be improved to provide safe and comfortable variable use for residents. A maintenance programme will also be instigated.

FROM ABOVE: Street front perspective; rear perspective; site plan

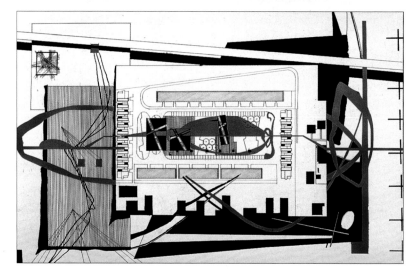

THE 'DRIBBLE' – CATALYTIC URBAN STRUCTURES
Piestany, Slovakia

Let us consider the macrocosm of architecture, the city, where the biological and the mechanical become interwoven. If we assume that the city is a hybrid timepiece, hive and amoeba, how do we treat it? Architecture in this context can be a type of mechanical surgery; a bridge, for example, a butterfly clip holding together areas of truncated communication.

Architecture and urban planning must relieve aneurisms in the veins and arteries of the city to facilitate the capillary action that the nucleus has on outlying areas. The noise of centrality attracts many more people and generates much motion. Circulation systems in the city should allow quick enjoyable routes to urban nodes. If this is not achieved, cities as they become older are inflicted with functions dependent on existing infrastructure and this additional loading causes a type of urban cholesterol; this then starves the nucleus of contact with the periphery and results in the truncation of the previously useful and the previously relatively adjacent. This causes a

long lingering brain death.

Architecture must be more infiltrative in its nature. It must exploit unfamiliar situations, enabling solutions and mixing uses at many disparate scales. Architecture can be used as a catalytic virus, penetrating the nucleus forcing space, or coordinating the Brownian motion of the population; buildings can be used as filters, funnels and deflectors. Urbanism is architecture's most virulent strain. It is not beautiful in the first aesthetic sense but in the second aesthetic, that is its potential catalytic action.

Piestany, Slovakia is an area whose major resources are therapeutic spas and a riverside cultural centre. This *Kulturforum*, featuring an art gallery and theatre, is set on the periphery of an urban park. The town centre, however, was apart from this area, and the opportunity for promenading, art-watching and noise-receiving was impaired. The proposal was to provide an enabling mechanism, to take the form of a 'dribble' of interventions that enhances existing functions, fine-tuning them and

facilitating new ones, that connected with the town centre across the park.

In the next decade the Slovakian metamorphosis will accelerate as new previously unallowed, or not foreseen, functions will jockey for space in the nucleus of the city. It is hoped that through the catalytic injection of these low-key urban additions the centre will be elongated, directing and deflecting the human corpuscles to areas of oral, aural and visual gratification. Functions are pulled and extruded from other buildings, a type of tectonic pocket-picking. An Art Wall was constructed and encouraged or cossetted art marks, but allowing the population to compete in the process of identification, by making its own art and placing it on this altar to *laissez-faire*.

Disparate elements and ideas have been brought together in Piestany to see whether this combination will transform into a set piece of urban 'gold'. Providing nodes outside the urban nucleus is beneficial and offers alternative foils for acting out life's absurd ritual.

Art Wall

64   Bosnia

IVAN STRAUS

ARCHITECTURE AND BARBARIANS
Diary of a Sarajevo Architect

This excerpt is from the diary kept by architect Ivan Straus between September 1991 and September 1992. Originally published in French (Ivan Straus, *Sarajevo, L'Architecte et les Barbares*, trans Mauricette Begic, with an introduction by Francois Chaslin, Edition du Linteau, 1994) it has now been published in Bosnian in Sarajevo (International Peace Center, 1995). It has been specially edited and translated from Bosnian by Aleksandra Wagner for *AD*.

I never wrote a diary before, not even in high school when that was considered normal . . . I mean – I have no experience with diaries. The decision to start in September of 1991 came with the first days of my retirement. I thought of writing it as an architect's testimony of 40 years of building and thinking about architecture. My timing, however, didn't allow for this topic only. The destruction of Croatia, and with it the destruction of much of what my generation has built, the destruction of Bosnia and Herzegovina – how could I have remained silent about it in my diary, how could I pretend that it has nothing to do with my life, as if I were under a glass bell? So my diary had a parallel theme; what wanted to be a record of building, page by page increasingly became a record of destruction . . . The time of destruction to which I was a witness, one witness among many, was horrible, unbelievable for an architect who watched his own and his colleagues' buildings go up in flames. Aggression, of course, doesn't stop there. Its brutality has to be recorded, not just by historians, writers, journalists, professional chroniclers – all citizens have an obligation to write a diary of their own.

1 October 1991 *Thinking again about architecture in the Socialist Federal Republic of Yugoslavia, a country that no longer exists, about the architecture which I have followed closely for many years and about its future within the 'former' geography, I have no choice but to remind myself that architecture always was the most expensive of arts. It is becoming more so every minute, and soon only very rich countries will be the carriers of architectural development in the domain of high technology and the aesthetics that are derived from it. Poor countries will be left with a secondary role of designing within the tradition and folklore of their own, with a role that will follow, complement or 'refresh' the world's architectural scene. Even that will not be possible for all. Our building practices will remain on the periphery of European events. I remember saying this in June of 1991, in an interview given for Belgrade radio. Why – I asked then – would architecture in Yugoslavia be any more profound than our current political, social, economic position in*

Europe? And I do mean architecture in Yugoslavia *and not* Yugoslav architecture, *because I have never believed in the 'national' concept in architecture. For me, architecture is an embodiment of civilisational encounter, of worlds, ideas, philosophies, of life itself. If there is a discipline within which the notion of universality is immanent, then it is architecture. If it wasn't so, why would anybody allow the Pompidou Centre to be built by an Englishman and an Italian, why would a Dane get to build an Opera house in Sydney, and how would architects from Norway win a competition for the Alexandria Library? One can certainly choose to think in terms of mimicries, one can wish to remain invisible in his or her given contexts, but that was never my choice. Herein lies the paradox; while architecture obviously was never 'dangerous' for socialist realism – at least not on our territories – and, I would also argue, only because nobody really understood architectural language, my first works and the works of many of my colleagues followed the ideas of the International Style. Its concept of beauty and function was taken as a conscious reaction to the prevalent dogmatic thinking about art and culture in general. But this, too, has to be surpassed – for it can only lead to mediocrity and uncreative parodies. To be an architect is to strive for spaces which inhabitants still need to conquer in order to feel good, in order to work and to live; it is to give a form to human demands and needs, to attract, enrich and relax, to contribute to human thought and to the idea of personal freedom; to make one aware of participating in one's own history.*

24 March 1992 *For a person like myself, whose thoughts and actions in architecture are fully conscious of both time and space, a letter from Boris Pecenko, a friend and colleague from Maribor, [Slovenia] was a happy moment in this craziness. He has replied to the package with my book on* Architecture in Yugoslavia 1945-1990, *sending these words of encouragement:*

> *I sincerely hope, regardless of the present situation, that we will keep in touch and continue to collaborate in architecture. It doesn't matter how it is going to be called – a Balkan or a South European one . . .*

Was it a gleam of light at the end of a tunnel?

22 April 1992 *We've spent a horrible night in the cellar. The noise outside made us think that everything our 'liberators' didn't like was concentrated on this street of ours. Only in the morning did we see their 'heroic deeds'. We spent all day cleaning the street of shattered glass, wishing to retrieve self-respect . . . And it was only a day or two ago that we watched on television the grand opening of the*

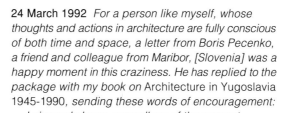

OPPOSITE, FROM ABOVE:
'. . . barbarians have decided to burn one of the towers of the business centre . . . the UNIS towers are turning into black, burned grids against the sky. . .'
Sarajevo, looking west, the burning Elektroprivreda building in the foreground; the UNIS towers ablaze, July 1992;
ABOVE: Ivan Straus, Unis, Sarajevo, 1986; and Elektroprivreda, Sarajevo, 1978

Seville Exposition called 'Discoveries' ... it was only two years ago that we had a competition – I was one of the members of the jury – where an excellent work by Zagreb colleagues, architects Marijan Hrzic, Tomislav Odak and Branko Siladjin was chosen as a project for the Yugoslav pavilion, for Seville.

8 June 1992 *It was three o'clock in the morning when we came up, walked to the apartment, and out on the balcony. A shock! – Tonight, barbarians have decided to burn one of the towers of the business centre in the Marijin dvor. The 'twins' have been already pretty well damaged, but one is burning now, starting somewhere on the eighth floor, and all the way up. It hurts me so, but I am trying to hide it: what is the loss of a building compared with the sorrows that have spread all over Bosnia and Herzegovina? Yet I was horribly sad, as I looked at my towers: moments of planning and of the construction went by with cinematic speed, as did my pride as maker – tonight it all burns like an immense torch. Nana, my wife, is consoling me. We are all alone on the balcony, this night and the next morning ... and all the following mornings while the UNIS towers are turning into blackened, burned grids against the sky.*

2 July 1992 *Today, for the first time in two months, I put on my suit and went into the city. A meeting was called concerning the activities of architects on the most important demolished buildings. On my way to the meeting and back, I walked slowly, seeing the city and its tragedy from a close-up perspective; it seemed a ruin after a cataclysm. To the human mind, unburdened by trivialities offered by this or that nationalism, the whole thing seems unexplainable. Can this devastation lead to some noble goal? Can it really be anybody's idea to divide Sarajevo once it is turned into a ruin? Absurd!*

27 July 1992 *Here I am, in hot Zagreb weather, waiting for my visa for Switzerland; alone on a journey to see my children and my granddaughter. My wife had to stay in Sarajevo: she is a Muslim, and Muslims cannot get the papers to leave. It is damn difficult to be a Bosnian today, in Bosnia as well as abroad. On the way here I learned about the sad destiny of another building I had built in Slano, near Dubrovnik. Met friends, Sarajevans in exile, professional colleagues. It was only in the evening that I remembered how 27 July used to be a national holiday in Bosnia and Herzegovina, the day which marked the beginning of its resistance in World War II. It became one of those dates when awards were given out. I received mine in 1978 – for a 'significant contribution' to the development of architectural thinking and practice in Bosnia and Herzegovina. I believe that the generals who are killing our cities today were the first to forget both the meaning of that day and of everything that was connected with it.*

5 August 1992 *After four days in Switzerland, trying like a mad man to reach my wife by telephone, listening to the bad and discouraging news, I am reading my first Belgrade paper in several months. No matter how much, and how much more we might have expected from Belgrade intellectuals, it is still a bit of encouragement to read a critical voice*

coming from them. This is what Nenad Stefanovic wrote in the May issue of Vreme:

> *While looking at the pictures of today's Sarajevo, desperately trying to recognise in the ruins places you once knew and loved, you can't avoid imagining the sick types who, on some hill, in cold blood, fill their cannons assured that by turning the city into a corpse, by destroying everything that lies below them – they are fulfilling the most honourable national task. Another image comes to mind, too, seen on a Belgrade television after Vukovar was liberated (from Life) in a similar manner: a 20-year-old 'liberator' fills his cannon with a shell and then, without any particular goal, pulls the trigger and sends his weapon somewhere in the direction of the city ... When politicians without brains and soldiers without education finished their job around Vukovar, it was made public that about 80,000 shells had fallen on this once-a-city. What was made public as well are many other facts which will ensure this 'liberation' a permanent place in the history of human dishonesty and militaristic stupidity. After Vukovar, according to the same logic – we built it, we will destroy it if necessary – came Dubrovnik, Osijek, Karlovac, Sarajevo, Mostar, Foca ... In both of these wars, in the pits of primitivism, has vanished, or is vanishing this very minute, what will be impossible to restore: valuable monuments, whole communities, the spiritual and the civilisational heritage of people who used to live here.*

26 August 1992 *What happened tonight is the most extreme peak of barbarity, or the pit of hell. After five months of merciless killing of Sarajevo, terrorists, those primitive fools from the hills, have burned Vijecnica, the National and University Library. For almost a century this was a built symbol of the modern city. Many buildings have burned in these five months – public institutions, residential blocks, schools and sports halls, religious and cultural monuments – but this fire that comes from Vijecnica is worse than anything ... As the Library burns, and as snipers are firing on those who are trying to save what can be saved, blackened pages of books are carried on the mild wind, uphill and downhill, across the city. Whose works were printed on those pages, whose poetry and whose prose, whose tragedies and whose humour? Ever since 1945 we have learnt about the burning of the National Library of Serbia – destroyed in the German bombing of Belgrade in 1941 – and we thought that we were learning about one of the most drastic losses. Here and now, there is another loss – for the generations to come.*

27 August 1992 *In the Sarajevo magazine Nedjelja [22 July 1992] an article was published by the architect Bogdan Bogdanovic, who is a conscience of the Serbian people as much as Zola was for the French during the Dreyfus affair. I have to quote it here, at least partially, for it will never lose a bit of its wisdom and accuracy:*

> *I am thinking about one among many abnormalities of the present civil war and I cannot comprehend the military doctrine which sets*

OPPOSITE, FROM ABOVE:
Perspective section, plan and elevations of the Unis tower reconstruction; exterior perspective of the Elektroprivreda reconstruction. Lebbeus Woods is working with Ivan Straus on these projects

as one of its first, maybe even as the first goal – destruction of the cities. The civilised world will, sooner or later, shrug its shoulders with indifference when thinking of our slaughter – and what else can it do? – but for destruction of the cities we will not be forgiven. We will be remembered – this 'Serbian side' – as destroyers of cities, as the new Huns. The horror of a Westerner is easy to understand: for centuries already, he does not distinguish, not even etymologically, between the notions of city and of civilisation. This senseless destruction of cities he cannot, therefore, understand but as a manifest, aggressive revolt against the highest values of civilisation.

Let's not forget the most diabolical of circumstances: what is at stake here are beautiful, very beautiful, the most beautiful cities: Osijek, Vukovar, Zadar, now Mostar and Sarajevo. The attack on Dubrovnik – I am horrified to say – was aimed at a specimen of exceptional, even symbolic beauty . . .

City-haters and city-destroyers are not bookish facts any longer. They are phantoms which are alive. They are among us. We are left to wonder from which depths of a disturbed national soul they were hatched, and where it is they are heading. What kind of morbid picture-book are they leafing through? It is obvious that the books they use are not the idyllic album of city memory . . .

20 September 1992 *There isn't a building of any significance in Sarajevo that hasn't been destroyed or damaged. Many of them were works of architects dating to the Austro-Hungarian period – Josip Vancas, Karl Parik, Aleksandar Wittek, Ciril Ivekovic, Rudolf Tonnies . . . the buildings and ideas of the period between the two World wars – of architects like Helen Baldasar, Dusan Smiljanic, Mate Bajlon, Muhamed and Reuf Kadic . . . as well as those from after 1945, buildings by Juraj Neidhardt, Zdravko Kovacevic, Halid Muhasilovic, Zivorad Jankovic, Namik Muftic, Bogoljub Kurpjel, Branko Bulic . . . Transportation and infrastructure have fallen apart, electricity and running water are absent for months at a time . . .*

We will need at least a decade – and only in case of good finances – to rebuild and restore big residential areas, hospitals and schools. For years, whether they want it or not, governmental institutions will have to work in improvised, small, non-representative spaces, while businesses – from banks to shops – will be renovated in accordance with their owners' resources. It will be an incredibly expensive, difficult and responsible task, in which every move will have to be made wisely and realistically, for hardly anything humans do is as prone to mistakes and malpractice as are building and rebuilding. Speed cannot serve as an excuse for mistakes . . . with so many ruins, buildings that were burned, with so much heavy damage, one will have to estimate with utmost care both the cultural and historical significance of objects to be restored and the economic reasoning behind each decision. What Sarajevo needs, obviously, is not only professional, but political wisdom. It is not simply a city now. It is more than that: a symbol.

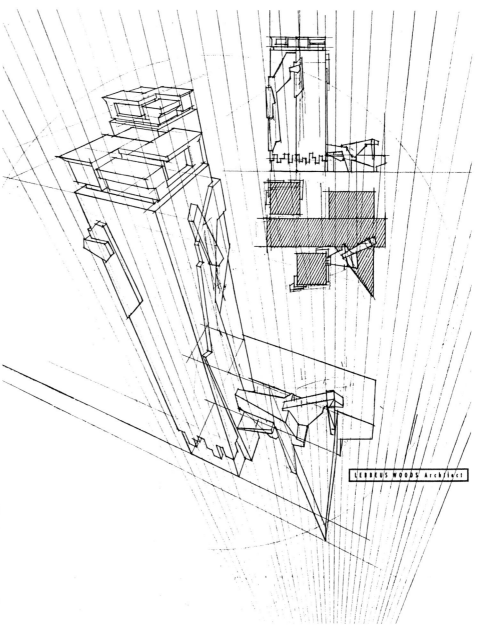

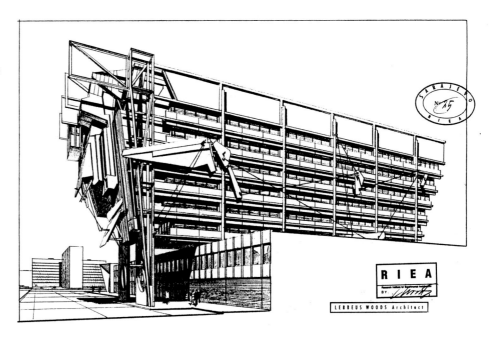

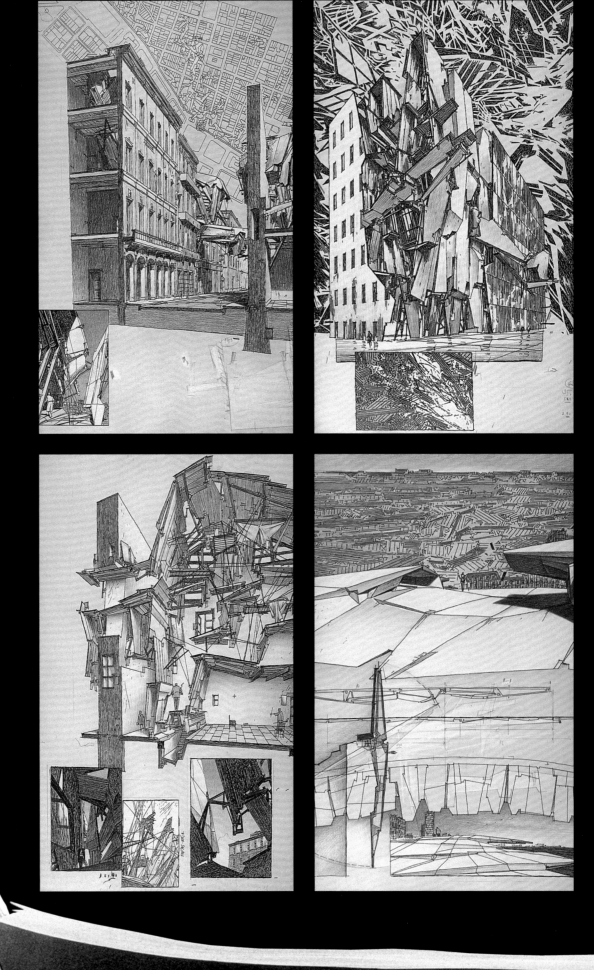

FROM ABOVE, L to R: Havana: The Wall, new houses on Monserrate, interior perspective section; Meta-institute, section perspective; new house on Monserrate, interior section perspective; Malecon, new seawall/shore, composite view; Malecon, model of the seawall/shoreline at flood tide

LEBBEUS WOODS
WALLS

Contemporary culture is in the midst of a crisis that can be met fully at its peripheries and edges, but not at its core, even though that is where its causes and most fatal effects are to be found. While at the core it is so effectively disguised, towards the boundaries of the culture, which are always to some degree neglected or at the limits of control from a centre of authority, the disguise slips somewhat, and the crisis is revealed.

The disguise is not simply an effect of the crisis, but a primary cause. Some essential reality is being masked by what has been referred to as the 'self-satisfaction' of mass culture, which is maintained at the expense of a creativity that emerges only from an imagination stirred by confrontation with every kind of experience and actuality. Crisis arises from the confrontation of disparate realities, when things of different orders meet and contend. However, through the predictable entertainments by which the world's growing number of consumers feel they are in touch with themselves and one another, and the fashions in everything from clothing to buildings which give a reassuring illusion of cultural differences and vitality, or the politicians and parties who promise the 'masses' more and more empowerment with less and less effort on their part, consumers are in fact encouraged to suppress their inherent differences and conform. This serves well enough the 'others' who thrive on consumers' dependencies, but reduces consumers themselves to a type of passivity that is historically new. It is the passivity described by Aldous Huxley in *Brave New World*, when he wrote that the way to control people is not with pain (the *modus operandi* of the police state), but with pleasure. What was once a privilege to be won now becomes a right to be demanded and received. The consumer waits to be pleased and in this way is continuously pacified.

The maintenance of this passive state is possible only in the absence of crisis, simply because crisis throws things off balance and forms an unpleasant, yet dynamic state. The crisis of consumer culture, then, is that it pretends there is no crisis, or at least none *here*. Crisis exists somewhere else, in black ghettos and the Balkans, and there it will be contained, either by the police or a peace-keeping contingent. The 'fall of Communism', symbolised by the tearing down of the Berlin Wall, has been proclaimed not merely as the triumph of the Western powers over the East, but as the victory of the Western way of life. Now there can be a Disneyland in Dresden, a Mafia in Moscow, and Everywhere a predictable Sameness. Everywhere but at the edge.

The projects presented here for Sarajevo and Havana propose in various forms a number of peripheries and edges commonly referred to as 'walls'. These most primordial of architectural elements do not simply separate other spaces, but define spaces within themselves, spaces 'between', zones where the norms and conventions of living on either side of the wall's divide do not or, more likely, cannot apply. These are zones existing in every city where crisis is inevitable. They are not simply outlaw zones, feeding on themselves, but the critical edges of urban life and culture

as a whole. They may be a university campus or an ethnic ghetto, or, at a geopolitical scale, an entire city or nation, which has found itself between abrading or colliding ideologies or cultures. These zones of crisis are the only places where actualities of the dominant culture are confronted, and from which new ideas essential to the growth of that culture can emerge.

This wall is metaphorical, but it can also be literal. In the latter case, it acquires an immediate tectonic presence, and at an architectural scale, may become a room, a street, or a city. Alternatively, the wall may become pure space, or, the negation of architectonic mass and materiality, and of the comforting assurance of their cause-and-effect certainty.

There are always people who will come to inhabit the difficult spaces of the wall. They are the people of crisis, pushed unwillingly to confrontation with limits, borderline cases of all kinds, the adventurers, criminals, inventors, con-artists, opportunists, the people who cannot, or have not been allowed to, 'fit in' elsewhere. They are nomads of the body, refugees of the mind, restless, itinerant, looking without much chance of finding a sure way either forward or back. Instead, they turn the situation to an advantage, making uncertainty a virtue, and strangeness an ally.

The architect of the space within the wall does not make predictive designs. Rather, he produces evocations which, however precise and detailed, are intended only as heuristic aids, guides indicating ways of reforming the space that will stimulate transformations by others. These productions cannot rely on the conventions that serve well enough elsewhere, so geometries and methods of construction are invented, provoking new ways of moving or resting in space, new and always transforming relationships between both people and things.

The High Houses designed in 1994 for Sarajevo reclaim not only a site destroyed by the siege of the city (the former tobacco factory near the centre), but also the space above, invisibly scored for three years by the arcs of shells, bullets and grenades that at the time of writing are still falling. These houses respond to a powerful need of people to achieve a freedom of movement in space through a fuller plasticity of experience, and to exist in the full dimensionality of space, to fly and yet, paradoxically, to be rooted, to belong to a particular place and time.

The war of aggression and attrition waged against Sarajevo aims to destroy not only its defences, but also its cosmopolitan nature. The Parliament buildings in the Marijin dvor, near the city centre, as strong symbols of urbanity, have been especially targeted and as a result damaged so severely that they are today abandoned. The reconstruction of these buildings, when it comes, cannot simply restore the former bureaucratic forms, either of space or of governance. The war has changed everything, and, most critically, the structure of society itself. The design for a new Parliament (1994) projects a 'meta-institute', consisting of an non-deterministic network of spaces woven in and through the surviving, homogeneous Cartesian framework. Leaving behind the principle of

PAGES 70/72:
War and Architecture
Series: Meditation;
THIS PAGE:
Meditation;
PAGE 74/75, ABOVE,
BACKGROUND:
New tissue construction;
INSET, L TO R:
Scar construction;
Injection construction;
new tissue construction;
Scar construction;
BELOW:
Bosnia Free-State: The
Wall, detail of elevation

hierarchy (a strictly 'vertical' system of organisation, working from the top down), and using in its place that of *heterarchy* (incorporating both vertical and 'lateral', fully three-dimensional systems), the new place of government will concern itself with its own reformation in relation to the inevitability of permanent social, economic and political change.

The outbreak of war in the former Yugoslavia in 1991 coincided with the development of projects for Berlin and Zagreb which introduced the 'freespace' and 'free-zone'. These concepts challenge canons based on building types and prescriptive (actually coercive) design. In their place is an architecture fully conceived in plastic terms by the architect, but evolved through successive interpretations by builders and inhabitants. The war's violence compelled a deeper examination of these concepts based on the relationships and interdependencies existing between violence and creativity, destruction and construction. The War and Architecture series consists of drawings which are meditations on this subject (itself a little-inhabited border area), and designs proposing a critical approach to the reconstruction of 'volatile', war-damaged sites. The proposed *injection*, *scab* and *scar* concepts of reconstruction are based on the principle of 'building on the existential remnants' of war, as a way to transform and transcend violent change.

As a result of several trips to Sarajevo both before and during the period of the siege, the opportunity came to work on specific reconstruction projects. The Elektroprivreda building and the UNIS towers (both corporate headquarters), designed by Ivan Straus, were seriously damaged by shelling and fire, though largely maintain their structural integrity. While the continuing siege makes any construction impossible presently, Straus is preparing designs for rebuilding, and requested collaboration. Together with proposals for damaged apartment blocks made during 1994, these projects extend the earlier research in the design of atypical spaces and programmes of use (freespaces), and of spaces at the peripheries of existing buildings (walls).

Havana, Cuba may seem a long way from Sarajevo, but in many ways it is not. The 'subject' of a social and political revolution 35 years ago, and since then the object of a trade embargo because this revolution was Communist, Havana is a highly-cultured, multi-ethnic city struggling to survive a protracted economic and political siege. It is a city in decay, if not in ruins, populated by people who live with dignity in spite of the indignities forced upon them. Another similarity with Sarajevo is in the approach to urban planning and architecture. During the past 35 years, the Cuban government had to turn to the countries of the Eastern bloc, including the former East Germany and Yugoslavia, for economic and technical assistance in building social housing, schools, hospitals. Socialist building types, construction methods and also the centralised approach to urban planning became the models adopted by Cuba. Not only that, but apartment blocks were prefabricated in Yugoslavia and shipped to Havana for assembly. The resultant drab conformity is much the same as in Eastern Europe (there is not such a difference, after all, between the consumer and the proletarian). The intense contrapuntal rhythms that mark Cuban culture as unique are mocked by the grey sterility of this imported architecture, yet in a way not so different from Sarajevo, where the cultural mix of East and West is equally unique and subtle.

After the 'collapse' of the Eastern bloc, all contact with these countries has lapsed, and Havana exists now in a state of suspension, and suspense, between ideologies, histories, and futures. It shares with Sarajevo the difficult fate of being in crisis, and, also, of being a critical edge whose importance reaches far beyond its geographical limits.

As a result of visiting Havana early in 1995 to attend a conference on architecture and urbanism organised by the *Museum fur Angewandte Kunst* in Vienna at the request of Cuban architects, three projects were proposed. They, like the Sarajevo projects, are conceived as labour-intensive rather than capital-intensive, producing an architecture corresponding to actual economic conditions, but also to an idea of the activity necessary in the zone of crisis, as opposed to the passivity of zones of the 'norm'. Here, new ideas and inventiveness are a necessity for everyone.

The first project is a new urban edge proposed for the Malecon, the wide six-kilometre-long boulevard forming a sharp northern edge with the Caribbean. An artificial 'shoreline' is constructed for recreational use, improving substantially on the narrow sidewalk and low sea-wall that now exists. It also forms a high and effective seawall when the force exerted by the flood-tide tilts it upright, protecting large portions of the city from the high tides of tropical storms and hurricanes.

The second project is proposed for the 'old city', the former Spanish colonial city founded in the 16th century that adjoins Havana's large, protected harbour. At present it is decaying, as there are no funds to restore the historical buildings, nor to maintain those built after Cuba's first revolution, which freed it from the colonial domination of Spain in 1902. With this in mind, a new urban wall is proposed along the line of the old city wall of the colonial period, in order to concentrate the energies in *Habana vieja*, intensifying processes both of decay and of growth. The Wall is a massive construction of masonry and concrete, containing utilities and serving as both a limit to, and armature for, the construction of new spaces within the old city. Constructed spontaneously of inexpensive, lightweight and versatile materials, 'function' is determined by idiosyncratic, and constantly changing, habitation.

Due to its vibrant culture and volatile political history, Havana is an ideal site for the establishment of an institution for the study of the idea and practice of institution itself. The aim of such a meta-institute is, as always, to devise principles, practices, and 'rules' by which institutions (social, political, cultural) can continually revise and reform themselves. But the institute proposed for Havana (explored in two versions) is devoted to the analysis and heuristic modelling of both stable and fluid urban terrain, the ambiguous, paradoxical and unpredictable landscapes of the contemporary city that embody both human and natural forces of change.

'Reconstruction Projects for former-Stabilities' might seem to be a more appropriate title for this group of projects to appear under than the present one. While it would not be untrue, it would not go far enough in revealing the underlying aspirations of the work. Perhaps the Bosnia Free-state project, a literal wall, reveals these best in its extremity and grandiose absurdity of scale. It 'defends itself' – survives, even flourishes – by absorbing all that comes its way, whether it is digitised information, or an invading army, whose artillery has little effect on its sponge-like, discontinuous and mathematically indeterminate structure, and whose soldiers lose their way in the seemingly disorderly sequence of spaces, settle in, and in so doing bestow an order. Cities have always needed a generous acceptance of the new, the strange, the unexpected, the upsetting and the disturbing. They need to engage the conflicts at their core, and today at a higher pitch of intensity, a more rapid tempo and at an unprecedented scale, but can only do this by engaging the crisis at their edges. The new walls to be built must, paradoxically, not only separate, but connect.

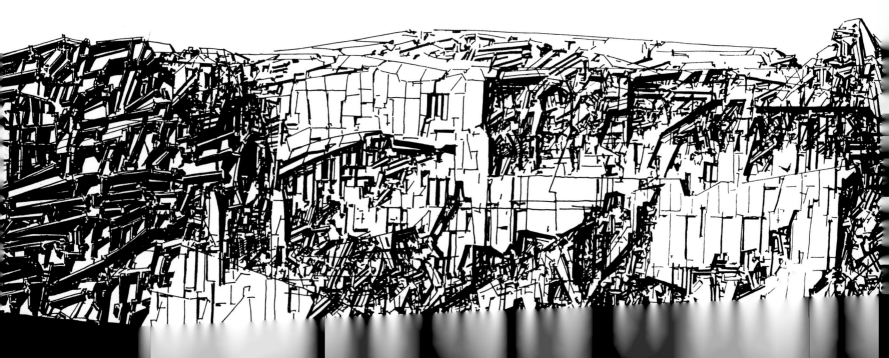

EXIT

EXIT HOUSE – LEARNING FROM BOSNIA
Mladen Jadric and Nevil Selimic

This house should be examined in the context of a garden city. Exit are trying to redefine the relationship of man – home and work, and house, city and nature. The basic idea is of a link between ecology and the new technological revolution of the return of work to the home.

Two world wars, huge speculations in land and real estate, the unscrupulous attitude towards nature, dilettantish and uncontrolled industrial development and the urban development of cities created more problems than solutions for a new generation of city planners. At the close of this century, we will be faced with two principles:
- reasonable co-existence with nature
- optimal relation between working and living space.

Exit house encompasses these two principles with a ground floor summer house and a first floor winter house.

The summer house

The basic elements of this house are the fence, the garden and the pavilion. This is a garden house, within which free development of three-dimensional space is possible. The open parts of the house represent 'rooms in nature' and they have a varied use. The closed parts of the house take up only so much of the space of the garden as necessary to satisfy the main functions of the house. In the organisation of the ground floor it is obvious that the definition between the external fencing and the walls of the house is disappearing. The walls move freely and successively spaces become open, half-open to closed, covered, half-covered to open.

It is possible to observe the architecture of the ground floor as only one of the many variants of space organisation according to the principle of movement.

The exterior wall encloses a part of nature and thus creates an urban oasis and transforms the parcel into a garden. This wall does not only serve the purpose of saving the 'city lungs', it also secures the complete intimacy and privacy of the inhabitants.

The openings on the exterior wall have very specific roles. The largest and main opening is the entrance gate. Towards the outside, it opens into the private and the public working part of the house, while in the backyard it regulates the connection between these two components as well as the link between the entrance and the covered yard.

The neighbour gate, namely the door between two plots, is a concept which relies on good relations between neighbours. We have to reaffirm the concept of neighbourhood in order to be able to deal with the social duties of life in a community.

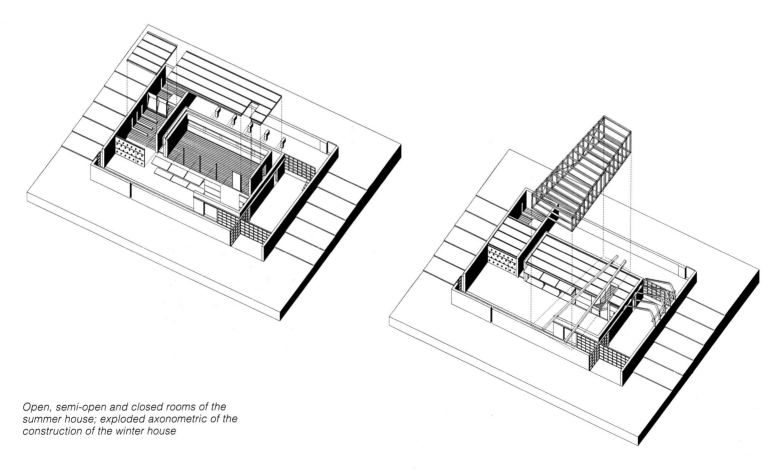

Open, semi-open and closed rooms of the summer house; exploded axonometric of the construction of the winter house

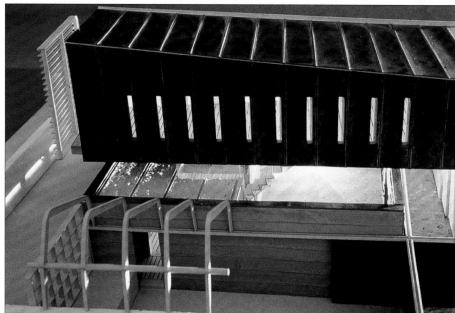

A further step in that direction is the affirmation of water for general use. A well-meaning householder will share water with his co-citizens by making a two-way drinking fountain. Those houses which have a garden beyond the walled enclosure will also have a fourth orifice, namely the exit to the garden, which is again connected to neighbouring gardens, emphasising that circulating between houses is possible without expensive highways and roads.

The interior wall moves to create 'open' (green, stone and similar) rooms which can be transformed into closed spaces at any time, according to the needs of the inhabitants, the structure of the family, financial possibilities and so on. The house opens and closes, an indeterminate enclosure because it develops towards the outside within its defined membrane.

The work area of the house was left 'unfinished' and can be used in different ways as a work space, a shop, or simply as a part of the yard, and in specific cases, as a garage. By its character and use of building material, it takes over the aesthetic of the 'public' part of the house. The covered areas of the house are formed as 'rooms without furniture'.

All living spaces are facilitated with essential installations; each of the rooms can satisfy sleeping, eating, living and working functions. In this way, one achieves an infinite number of combinations in relation to the number of inhabitants, seasons and conditions of work. The ground floor premises are called 'the summer house', because the house/garden is most in use during the summer. The division of the house between 'summer' and 'winter' is a consequence of a continental climate where winters are harsh and summers hot.

Special attention is paid to the culture of water (bathrooms) and body care. The bathroom is expressed as an independent facility, with both open and closed space. The 'green rooms' are integrated with the house according to the principle: 'build and plant' and 'right to nature', as equal premises in the ground floor organisation.

The winter house

The first floor – the 'winter house' – is the 'public' part of the house, exposed, like the belvedere, and is situated in the garden. Originating from the principle of 'right to a view', this pavilion in nature developed as a result of the merging of two occurrences – the right to have sun on one side and the view to the city on the other. The lateral sides of the winter house: one is completely open and diaphanous towards the house; and the second, working part, is of a more closed character and construction. From the 'winter house' it is possible to see the city, surroundings and garden.

As on the ground floor, all of the rooms can be functionally interchangeable. The geometry of the orifices as windows onto the outer world has defined the form of the pavilion. Towards the city – a sweeping panorama of the city, towards the gardens and the hill an elevated view, which captures the sun.

The 'city' and the 'garden' room is the *divanhana* – a room which would be a meeting place of the household members, oriented exclusively toward the yard. The *divanhana* is a concept which is unfamiliar in the European house. This room functions as a living room, in a humorous and modest way (if we can use the concept of a living room in this type of house).

The proportions are defined by the principle 'A house to suit the master', and they allow individual spatial qualities. Mobile stairways enable different circulation through the house. It is possible to separate different generations, meanings, even families, within one mutual house.

Curiosity and privacy are in accord with the semi-permeable openings which allow a view to the outdoors, but no indoor views. The possibility of shielding the view or the sun within the urban matrix is defined by very strict rules of conduct: 'right to a view' and 'right to the sun'. Thus by moving pavilions, a synthetic picture is obtained of the democracy of urban groupings and of their heterogeneous and explicitly non-hierarchical character.

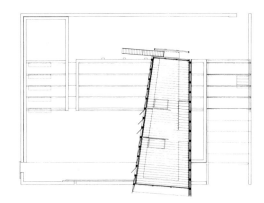

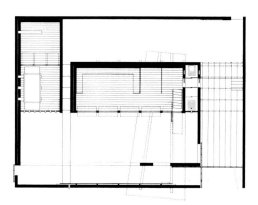

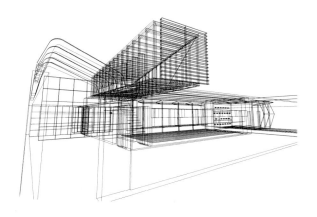

FROM ABOVE: Winter house plan; summer house plan; structural perspective

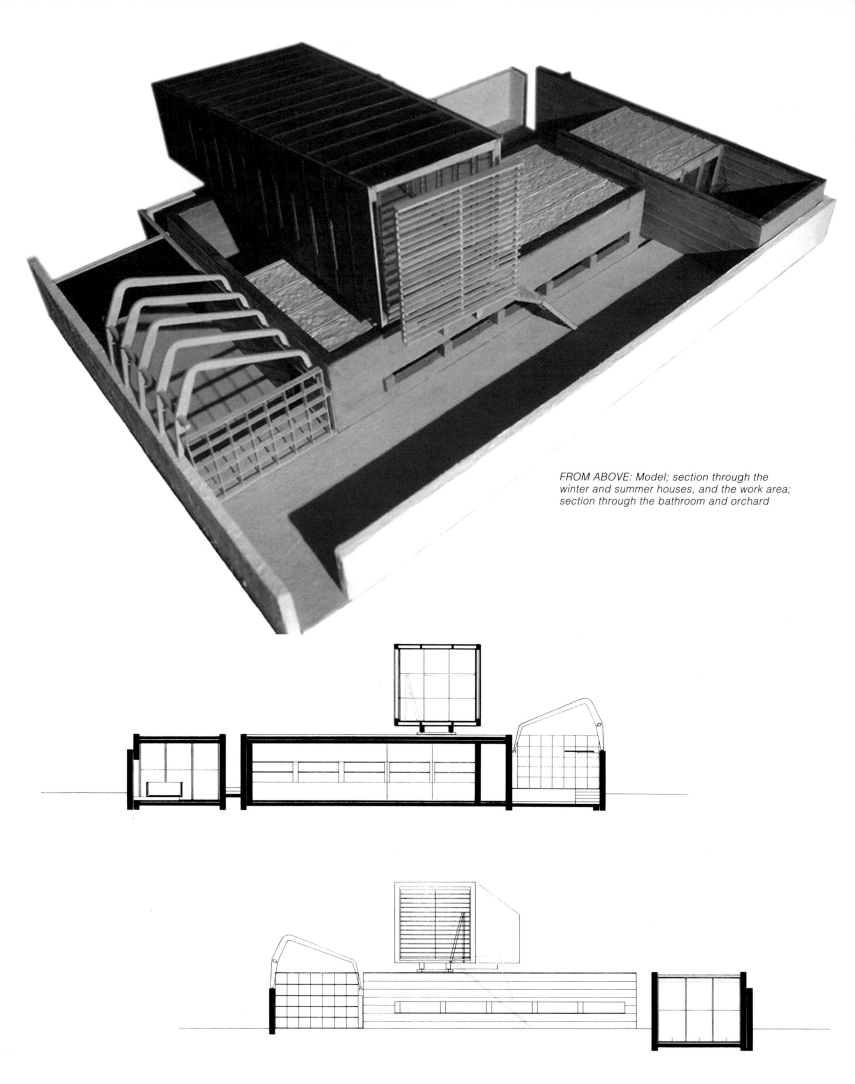

FROM ABOVE: Model; section through the winter and summer houses, and the work area; section through the bathroom and orchard

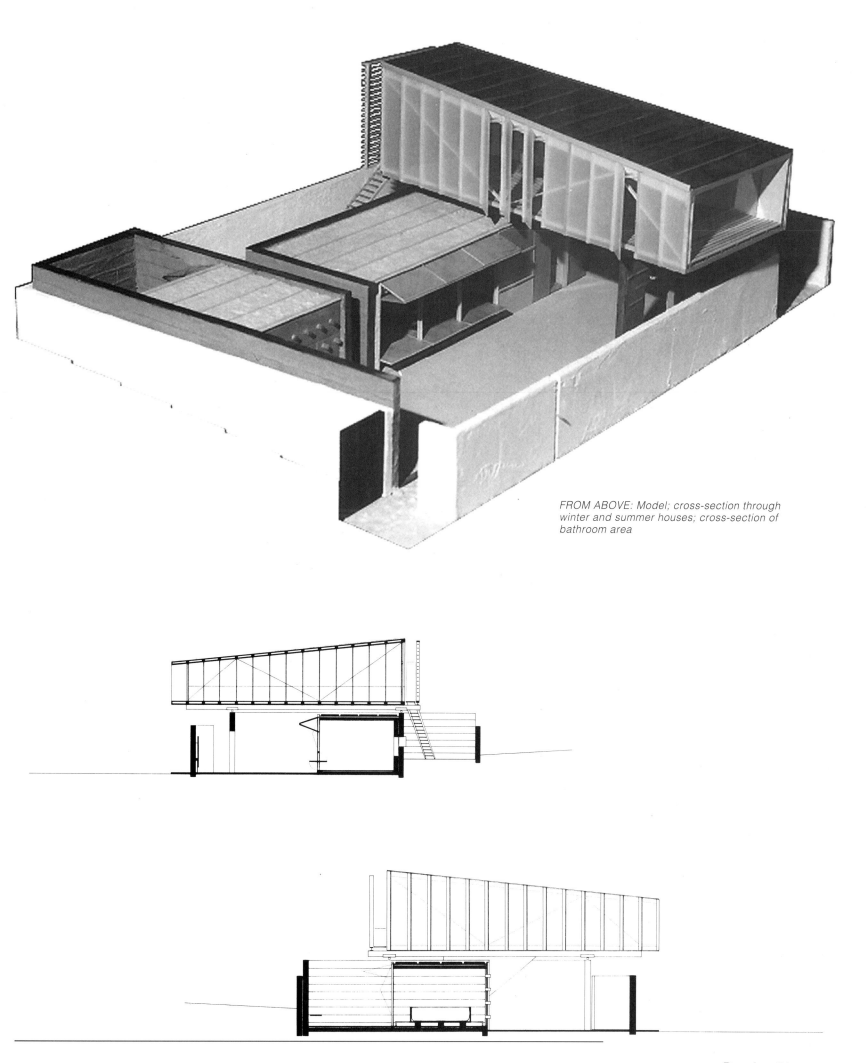

FROM ABOVE: Model; cross-section through winter and summer houses; cross-section of bathroom area

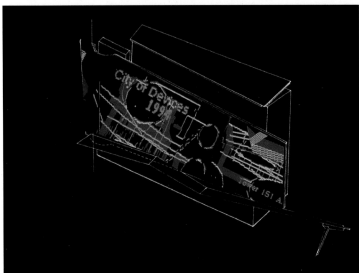

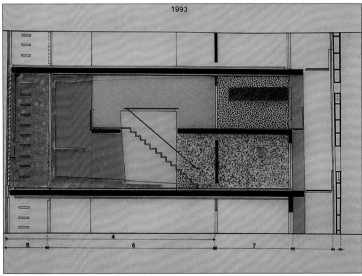

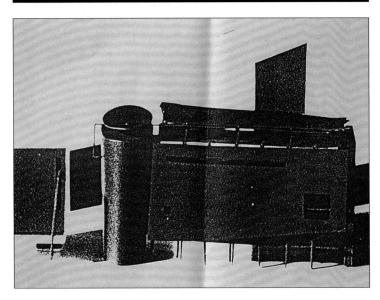

The City of Devices – A project of parts. The City of Devices *programme is a process in which the role of methodology and product are examined on the basis of a changing ideology and urban structure. Sigecica lies in the south-east quarter of Zagreb, north of the Sava river. This proposal invests in passive and active environmental control. The planning of the 1950s and 60s has left a mark in terms of 'object' (building) placement and the disjunction of pattern (plan) to these objects. This relationship establishes Vukovar as an edge to the land and to an incomplete urban block. The project thus acts as an edge and a barrier. The barrier is explored on the micro- and macro-level, becoming a component of environmental control and form. The north-facing screens of each block are designed as a composite sandwich, the skin being transparent. On the outer surface a constant flow of water cascades from the upper level to the roof of the commercial areas at street level, reducing pollution levels and allowing for a greater air circulation. The screens may be fitted with screen-printed duplex panels carrying advertisements for two products or companies simultaneously advertising. This would be a necessary element of the metropolitan home. ABOVE: Model of blocks A, B and C; CENTRE: the projection panel facing Vukovar Avenue, section through a typical apartment element; BELOW: an early view from the north, model. (Tower 151 Architects – Andrew Yeoman, John Cramer and Diana Kacic)*

ANDREW YEOMAN
A MODERN REVOLUTION – A HISTORY REVISITED

Taking the various statements of Marinetti and Gropius[1] into context, the Modern Movement was indeed a triumph of secular over spiritual belief, which spurred Nietzsche's mantra for the death of God.[2] This association of philosophical issues with that of the aesthetic and tectonic had its sceptics. Erich Mendelsohn made it clear that his inspiration from Bach was far superior to *Die Glasserne Kette* which concerned his fellow Berlin architects of *Arbeitrat fur Kunst* and specifically, the Dessau group from whom he became slowly estranged.[3] Such conflict in architecture is perhaps quite remarkable if one considers the banal ethos of current trends in the profession whose concerns over Continuing Professional Development (CPD) and the Nikkei Index have swallowed the art of theoretical posturing.[4] However the change of ideological status throughout Europe and the whole globe is of the shared phenomena of these two eras of 'Now' and 'Then', which to the casual observer of architectural history might signal another launch of a Modern Movement. Many have tried before, with Post-Modernism, Deconstruction, Pluralism and now Sustainability. The desire to form groups as in a collective has ebbed over the decades with individual quality being overcompensated with style which endangers the collective and obstructs mutuality.

The original topic of this essay is by default hampered by history which is open to a definition fraught with truth and value and hence begs some reflection on this matter. Francis Fukuyama's essay 'The End of History'[5] concludes with a vision of our culture as nostalgia which serves a different purpose:

> The end of history will be a very sad time. The struggle for recognition, the willingness to risk one's life for a purely abstract goal, the worldwide ideological struggle that called forth daring, courage, imagination, and idealism, will be replaced by economic calculations, the endless solving of technical problems, environmental concerns and the satisfaction of sophisticated consumer demands.

This is an important point bearing in mind that the writings of Engels and indeed Marx have in essence been rubbished by the West in the collapse of the Union of Soviet Socialist Republics and its associated Eastern European demographics, leaving a vacuum in the origins of philosophies and, in essence, ideology for both East and West. The free range of capitalism, or more accurately a version of monetarism,[6] is moving with the tide without more than a little fraudulence to hinder it. Kenneth Frampton recently announced the victory of capitalism during a workshop in Zagreb which was aimed towards the poignancy of theoretical premise and avant-garde principles over people[7] and again throws open the door to the discussion of what is an ideal in the contemporary world. Francis Fukuyama goes on to say:

> The triumph of the West, of the Western idea, is evident first of all in the total exhaustion of a viable systematic alternative to Western liberalism. If one consider the annals of social politics and culture on a shelf of which one end has collapsed, the last book on this collapsed shelve of ideol-

ogy could indeed be Huysmann's *Against Nature*, the story of aesthetic obsession borne by financial excess.[8] As environmental matters [sic] become a greater force in our social-politics the ideological tradition of politicking, which is having its last days seen out in the Balkans, the search of authenticity in truth and value may surface again.

Croatian architecture is derived, as in most European countries, from a series of imperialist, religious or demographic influences, be it from the Byzantine or Ottoman Empires, to Peter Behrens; all are represented in this new state. The status of 'beyond the revolution' is perhaps premature, as history, of course, is still being made (and simultaneously broadcast by CNN). Croatia has been a state for 900 centuries, albeit under another state's umbrella as in Austria and Hungary, or part of a federation as in Yugoslavia.

If there was a revolution then it was in 1971 when Croatian succession over central government in Belgrade forced the then Josip Broz (Tito) regime to permit separatist state ruling in Slovenia, Croatia, Bosnia, Montenegro and Kosovo. At a time when tourism in Croatia had generated a strong income for Yugoslavia, the expansion of the building industry by quasi-state developers had resulted, in many cases, in enormous conurbation projects of hotels and apartment blocks. Quality was not governed on aesthetic grounds in so much as its beauty was newness and not an antiquarian value which was, and is, bourgeois. Traditions were tolerated, as well as religion, which permitted mosques, Catholic and Orthodox churches to lie in close proximity to one another and provide what Western culture recognises as a traditional urban landscape. Such traditions of urbanity are found in Zagreb, though it also provides a safe seat for Modernism.

The city of Zagreb has been formed by a series of layers overlapping the centuries. In essence, the Habsburgs provided Zagreb with the scale evident in the downtown area and the city is clearly mapped chronologically from north to south, starting in Medvednica and culminating at Novi Zagreb. As a capital city the government is eager to construct all the icons normally recognised with such an identity. The Croatian legacy of architecture is not well known outside its boundaries although it carries a petulant locale of hands-on Modernism. In the summer of 1933 Wiessman and Antolic, two aspiring theorists and architects from Zagreb, not being able to afford the sea fare, took a train to Athens to join the ship on which CIAM was meeting. It was later established that some of the clauses in the infamous Charter document, drawn up by Le Corbusier, with a majority of French architects, were derived from the two young Croatians. The works of both these two architects, along with that of Galic, Ibler, Planic, Haberle and Bauer are now protected; albeit their actual physical conditions are in some cases appalling. The picture-book image of both La Ville Radieuse and the Unité d'Habitation is well represented and even, crossing the river to Novi Zagreb, the idea that wrought iron furniture and biplanes could be part of the scenery is almost plausible. The child of the Athens Charter, although one with curious spermizones. As

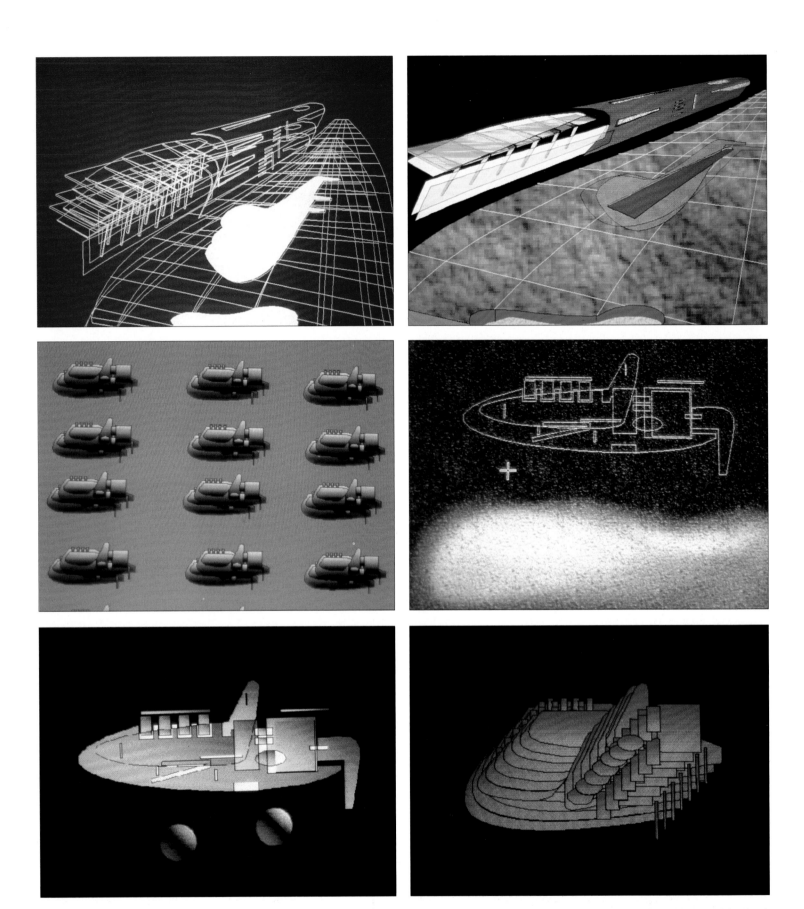

Zagreb Golf Club – an object in the landscape in which landscape is the pattern for the structure. Golf possesses a universal language and is clearly understood by the majority of the world's population. It is a sport which requires sophisticated hardware, a change of clothes and a change of attitude. Zagreb's Golf Club has never had its own course and it was proposed to develop a site on the northern bank of the Sava river, which resembles a Louisiana swamp. The planning authorities stated that any building should be sympathetic to those along the Sava River. A difficult task: either mammoths like the old Viticís CCCP Headquarters or shanty town structures of old timber and truck parts. A jungle of old washing machines, the site began a sortie into the hallucinogenic world of Sergeant Pepper's Blue Meanies, Yellow Submarines and strange structures of perforated layers, as an animated comment on the affluent society. The genesis is illustrated by the scanned foetal element which developed as artificial fossils and with an introduction of mechanical devices began the form. The project is a series of literal and acquiescent layers, either in timber brise-soleil and stone wall or, in the composition of interlocking interior parts, as in a submarine. ABOVE: Submarine in landscape as frame network, the object and landscape; CENTRE: the foetal submarines, the fossil and etching; BELOW: foetal elements, studies of the hotel.(Tower 151 Architects with Studio A. Andrew Yeoman and Nenad Kondza)

a member of CIAM and CIRPAC, Weissman, a collaborator with both Le Corbusier and Adolf Loos, urged more cohesion with the institutions of the Soviet Union even after the purge of the avant-garde by Stalin in the late 40s and 50s. With the works of Chernikov being viewed as bourgeois by the Stalinist authorities, the avant-garde left the Soviet Union and with them went any connection that might have been possible with the 'Moderns'. Even after Weissman identified this as being the true Modern or social condition, albeit in its raw state, Novi Zagreb is by its scale and material an example of the true Modern fusion of the act of design with direct social engineering. Polemically, when CIAM retreated to America, such curators of design as Philip Johnson supported the International Style but loathed the social dogma that came with it. This might be seen as the end of Modernism as an ideal in terms of ideological principles. Coupled with Fordism in America the inherent improvement of the industrial process began to encourage a desire for technical perfection. It launched the style as primary and in fact was the vanguard to fashion as a replacement. CIAM purported to provoke social reform which allowed architecture a real cut of the construction business and provided a link for the architects to exercise power.

The urban phenomena was of civility and drainage, with the CIAM providing an international agreement of standard. It should be remembered that this came at a time of post-World War I desire for international harmony, be it through German re-industrialised programmes to the League of Nations (later the United Nations) or Roosevelt's New Deal. The embracing of global standards (in the Western hemisphere) became the norm and thrust architecture forward as the purveyor of the New Spirit. In Zagreb one gains an understanding that this was entirely possible; even now masters of this era are held up as templates and the teaching of function and standards is as rigorous as it would have been in the Bauhaus. This curious social constitution in which architecture participates: the simple placing of the kitchen close to the dining room and in Gropius's words, proclaiming 'the Home is the City', makes the social conscience now even more compelling. A simple observation of the dialectic function of an elevator in a public building serves to define the essence of that elitist axiom of 'public and private' which are constructed of ideals and ideology. Colin Rowe made this a different description of languages and volume which collectively creates the ambience. This language has been by its very syntax absent from the socialist environment of state centralised control. Privacy was/is the family and the social discourse of the group a necessary part of leisure. Work was work and holiday, a holiday, green grocers the very same.[9] Market skills, speculative investment, polemical debate, political debate even, was not an issue and even when entertained, created massive disadvantages for the individual. Permitted ownership was organised through state-mandated construction companies who were responsible for large apartment blocks in Zagreb. This was an act of privacy but with state rules. Ownership has now, in post-Gorbachev times, become the main issue. Property the state had acquired through a social programme of distribution or simple confiscation has been returned to original owners or certainly, this is the intention. Zagreb property rights have been absent for over half a century with many records of boundaries, house ownership and legal status of property remaining as it was in the 19th century. An almost feudal system of land rights exist in parts of the city which make it impossible for potential developers to consider future projects. This is perhaps a blessing in disguise as the *nouveau riche* arrive to construct

their own small Toronto or Frankfurt.[10] This is the reality which is current in Zagreb. However, as the act of ownership, and the self-governing status grow and in an absence of rent control, there are fears that inflated prices will cripple the economy.

Although the conflict which has enveloped the country and the region for four years has kept foreign investors away, there are pockets of new wealth which keep building. The rents in central Zagreb are extraordinary: the price of a shop in the new underground shopping centre is 8,000.00 deutschmarks per metre, equivalent to a shop on 5th Avenue, New York. The shops are very small and getting smaller. The large department store of NAMA, near the Square of the Republic, is a Baroque '70s-conversion nightmare' and is quite spartan in comparison to the exotic jewellery and perfume store at the base of a Peter Behrens building on the east side of the square (now named Ban Jelicica Trg). The jet set meeting the peasant. Zagreb's environment cannot be simply described, providing, as it does, a curious dialectic dispossession of the agrarian and urban. The new library is surrounded by small holdings where the owner keeps livestock. One must ask if this is so bizarre. Western European standards of patronage, configuration and mix are often cited as a baseline for future development but their appropriateness in a city which has a stock exchange without stocks, over-inflated company values and a financial infancy must be questioned. There is a vast catalogue of such observations which make one wonder what is possible. The absence of foreign financial input, however, does not necessarily mean an absence of desire.

A recent trip to St Louis in Missouri put this in perspective. Once known as the gateway to the West, it seems to have suffered a serious regression. Its famous 300-metre-high vaulted stainless steel arch is there to remind one of an historical past, but the railway station has become a giant restaurant, the trains now being a poor relation to air transport. The city has died, although its historical routes read as agnostic metaphor. Returning to Zagreb one again meets this symbolic gateway, though more veiled than in St Louis. Zagreb forms a transition point between East and West, where cultures meet and exchange is possible. In the 15th century, the Ottomans fell 50 kilometres short of Zagreb, after fighting a bloody battle at Petrinja, which is a site of further carnage today. Seen as the last city in Europe, or more accurately, Catholic Europe, the Vatican has the largest diplomatic residence here, which has recently been rehoused in a new 'Drive-in McDonalds' structure in the fashionable north side of town. It is a simply horrible building of truncated campanile and loggia set on a shopping mall plan which Pope John II had to consecrate for his cardinal. The diplomatic quarter is noticeably populated with police kiosks which guard the entrance of each house in Pantovcak, which are identical to the newspaper stalls on the main square.

New architecture is not so cynical and follows a variety of paths all quite recognisable and yet possessing an absence. There is the well executed Stirlingesque swimming pool of Penicic and Rogina. Constructed in 1985 when the two young architects were still in university, it allowed them to set up office and become independent. Milan Sosteric's project on Petrinska has the remarkable Tao of being Zagreb's most controversial building. Won in competition his design uses a vertical wing to cut both the building and the street, a singular device remarkable for its presence and size. Rako and Radonic were short-listed in the Nara competition of 1994 with a project which proposed the export of a design by Turina, one of Croatia's heralded Modernists, to be enclosed in a delicate envelope. Many [11] have found success in the

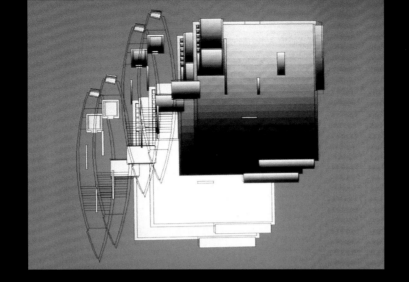

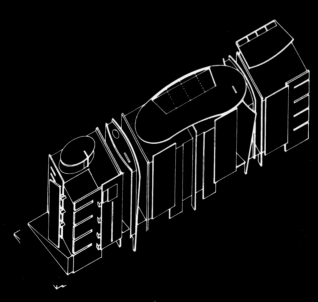

Martinovka – the urban interior as a room in which a series of devices lies; objects within a layered pattern. The series of development diagram scans is the beginning of the computerised file. Samples are taken of the existing, together with more global geometry and fuses in layers and later, in three-dimensions. This crude morphing of analytical form and metaphorical line provides a network for the formal qualities of the project and, in parallel, a further test of 'Devices' as urban object and junction. The project has now expanded in scale with an additional 3,000 square metres of commercial area and is currently at planning stage. ABOVE, CENTRE: A typical block (first 'Device' paintings); BELOW: Axonometric of

Europan competitions (II & III), in Germany, Austria (Penecic and Rogina) and Netherlands (Nirije and Nirije) and originally in Zagreb, Diana Kacic with her colleague Ljiljana Curcija. In fact, the architects of this generation ('59ers') share the same striving necessity as in Britain to be both famous and economically viable.

Many architects of my generation have set-up shop or simply gone to Austria to join growing communities both in Vienna and Graz. A reciprocal aspect to that of Victor Kovjecic and other Wagner pupils, who at the turn of century graced Zagreb with Secessionist structures. The Austrian influence is paramount in Zagreb though there have yet to be any little 'Himmelblaus', as noted in Klagenfurt, where most cafes have a flying wing or two. To answer a question concerning foreign influence it has to be clear on what terms this should be viewed. The architects of this country obviously come from various stables of both a regime with direct influence and an intelligentsia of prosperous thought. Talking to Sasa Lasso, the Modernism expert in Zagreb, it is clear that the rich heritage of the Secessionism, *L'Esprit Nouveau*, *Zeitgeist*, and *Werkbund* meets here. A visit to a Maxwell Fry building in Peckham some years ago did not evoke the same emotion as did the Galic apartment block on Avenija Vukovar, although both are in a similar state of poor maintenance. A visiting group from the Swiss Corbusier Foundation stated they found the Galic Unité to be an improvement on the master. A curious and certainly endearing observation.

To begin working in such a turbulent environment of war, financial chaos, cultural transition, political posturing and architecture mezzo one must not consider any of this if one is to remain both sane and functioning. Tower 151 architects shares an office in downtown Zagreb with its associated companies of Studio A and Investinzenjering. We are the new breed of multi-disciplinary, inter-flexible, quasi-architectural developers. With work in Denmark, Bulgaria, France and even Britain the politics are in check and the rich mixture of Modernist hardware and a fluid carpet of planning allows for the theoretical to be possible again. It is the Foucalt moment when chaos brings forth some clarity, albeit for a moment, before it plunges back into a cauldron of sudorific politicking and economics. The theoretical premise is the 'City of Devices' which was born in the age of Revolution, The Nova Gorica and Gorizia project developed as the same time the tanks of the JNA (Yugoslav Army) crushed the first Slovenian Zastava and then moved on to Croatia in 1991. We moved in its wake and arrived a few months after the first air raids in Zagreb. The programme of the 'City of Devices' provides a platform for strategic intervention in a city. It relies on point action, both economically and structurally and is levied at confronting the truisms of master planning. The series of projects currently 'on the drawing board' vary from a golf course to an experimental housing/commercial development. The 'event' as a replacement for the axiom 'public/private' is more appropriate as the structures develop from a process of analytical study based on the design of the mechanism, the 'Device'.

The confusion of ideology and representation which Kenneth Frampton identified in his critical essay on Modern architecture is indeed still apparent. I refer specifically to the term New Tradition which saw the abstract modernism supplanted by a conservative remodelling of traditional 'styles'. This is perhaps the point of confusion which Western Europeans, and indeed Americans, find in both the work of the Moderns and what is now contemporary. As was pointed out before, the commercial market of America embarked on the work of Mies, Gropius and Breuer by supporting the 'style' (see, for example, the work of Skidmore Owings and Merrill during the 50s and 60s and Philip Johnson's glass house as opposed to housing quarters of Philadelphia where social structure has collapsed). The misappropriation of style in absence of its ideological base may lead to such a cultural *melée* when a consumer society is expected to live in a social habitat. Of course the Japanese have found a compromise and the Modern we are discussing here can only be attributed to a European condition. Discussing this matter with a colleague recently we came to the conclusion that contemporary architecture had similar characteristics to 'Rock and Roll' and that fashion in architecture had surpassed that of politics as its concubine and fundamental source of inspiration, whereas 'Rock and Roll' had developed political overtures and, in many ways, corporate power. Bearing this in mind I turn to my *Tubular Bells* album and ask, who will lay claim to being the architectural Richard Branson (perhaps he/she already exists) and in turn, who will pen 'Anarchy in the UK', or is this simply history?

Notes

1 This refers to two addresses given by Marinetti and Gropius at different times which outlined, in the former case, the Futurist Manifesto, *La Splendour Geometrique et Mecanique*, (manifesto), Milan 1914 and the latter, the opening of the Bauhaus. *The New Architecture and the Bauhaus*, 1916.

2 This is a reduction of Nietzsche's notion that the coming of the mechanised world was a support to the Enlightenment, an overcoming of spiritual mysticism and the beginning of man's quest for control in all matters or 'will to power'. This was, in Nietzsche's view, the primary human drive which has encouraged many of the world's philosophers to seek the origins of this works and examine again Plato and Aristotle.

3 Erich Mendelsohn was by his own admission an outsider albeit contributing to the urban scene in Berlin. However the sad reality of being Jewish in a Fascist regime caused great rifts to occur including his exclusion from many exhibitions in the late 30s. It is perhaps ironic that he was one of the first German architects to visit America (becoming close friends with Frank Lloyd Wright) and later, the USSR, allowing him to make a vital comparison which would be apparent later in the century.

4 This is not a cynical stab at theory but an observation of how the theoretical has become hermetic, though when brought to bear in application develops unclear messages which are perhaps different from the intent of the origin. For example in Britain, community architecture became a small movement and even a specialised subject (RIBA list of architect's services). This questions the right of the architect to provide social architecture outside this titled and abbreviated condition, ie community architect. The polarity to this may be in the linguistic terms. See Robin Evans, critique of Peter Eisenman's work, 'Fin d'Ou T Hou S', *AA Files No 10*, March 1985, where the basis of Eisenman's use of structuralist linguistics and the assimilation with Chomsky and, later, Derrida, in one formal language of architecture, exposes the potential dangers of what has been seen as abstract in the corporeal sense of philosophy and theory.

5 Francis Fukuyama, *The End of History and the Last Man*, Extract published in 'The National Interest' 1989.

6 Milton Friedman provides a clear opposition to JM Keynes. The Keynesian policies of post-World War II became difficult to manage in the growing commercial economy of Britain and the more fiscal policy of monetarism became the primary structure. It demanded cuts in social services to offset low inflation and interest figures. However if one considers the strategies of property developers this might be viewed as being strictly Keynesian, if short term. See John Maynard Keynes, *The Economic Consequences of Peace*, 1930.

7 In April 1995 a workshop 'Frames of the Metropolis' was organised in Zagreb with guests Kenneth Frampton, Herman Hertzberger and Raoul Bunschoten. The issue of the abstract as a tool for planning was argued against planning for the people. Essentially, this pointed towards the use of abstract form and language in architecture, specifically in urban planning and its dialectic relationship with formal culture and philosophy, ie life, or hedonism.

8 The story of Des Esseintes and the desire to live in a world in which his own fantasies have priority. An interior is constructed which provides this and excludes all outside influences. This is perhaps one of the finest descriptions of the hedonist as both intellectual and madman, and one which has been read by many architects in their quest for the public /private discourse. JK Huysmann, *A Rebours (Against nature)*, 1959, translation.

9 There is a specific emphasis on the word 'Privat' (Private) as companies, shop owners and even institutions begin to pull away from the state system.

10 There is a large immigrant community in Germany and a high proportion of ex-patriot Croatians living in Canada.

MILAN SOSTERIC

RESIDENTIAL AND COMMERCIAL BUILDING
Petrinjska, Zagreb, Croatia

This building comprises apartments, offices, stores, catering businesses and parking lots, and is located in Petrinjska, the oldest street in Zagreb's Lower Town.

Petrinjska was developed as an access route to the city centre from the southern outskirts. With the most recognisable symbol of the city, the dome rising above the centre, and the predominant image of the spires of the cathedral above the roofline of the street, a clear and spatially dominant facade has been created which forms the greatest part of the visual aspect of the street.

At the same time, the building reconciles the two divergent styles of architecture present: the historic northern houses dating from the beginning of the century and the more modern southern ones dating from 1932. The console section of the house, which accentuates the semantic aspect, reconciles the two architectural worlds by clearly separating them and thus enabling a resolution of the facade which corresponds to both architectural expressions.

A courtyard located behind the building is filled with attractive stores, a parking lot and a children's playground, situated among chestnut trees.

Competition perspective drawing, 1992

LEFT: Competition sketch, 1992; ABOVE: West
elevation to the street; BELOW: East elevation

ATELIER LOEGLER & PARTNERS

A GATEWAY INTO THE CITY OF THE DEAD

Crematorium, Cracow, Poland

'Above all is the light,' Luigi Snozzi. Atelier Loegler's winning design for the 'Gateway into the City of the Dead' competition organised by the Cracovian chapter of the Association of Polish Architects (SARP) to design a funeral home for Batowice Cemetery, was based upon a desire to create a building which would be a timeless sign; a building which, as a 'gate' at the end of time, would be a symbol of the borderline between the worlds of life and infinity. The design was chosen to represent this idea: the passage from light into shade, the contrast between darkness and light, the problem of the individual experience evoked by the symbolic power of various forms.

The idea of creating an object of architecture which would become a simple sign, resulted in a choice of ascetic form and use of very simple materials – the stone of today, concrete and glass. The fully transparent front wall contrasts with the concrete and 'opens' the interior of the structure. The intermediate space, where the ceremony of dematerialisation of a human being is celebrated, is marked by a glass wall with dense metalwork – as a visual filter.

The structure is a functional whole. The various service areas are interconnected but preserve their unique character and the various groups participating in the whole cremation process have separate means of entrance.

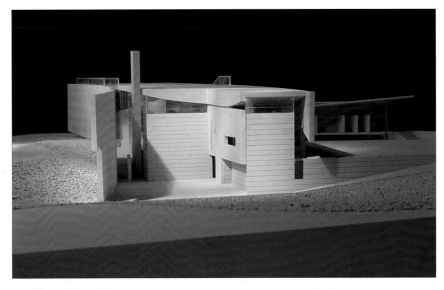

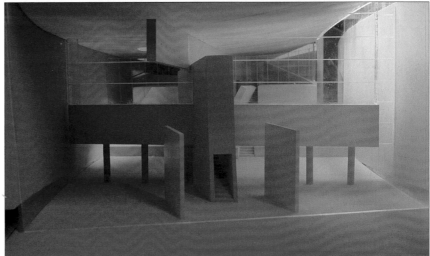

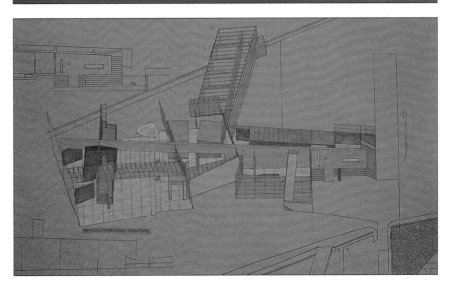

OPPOSITE, ABOVE and CENTRE: Views of model; RIGHT: Axonometric

ACADEMY OF ECONOMICS
Cracow, Poland

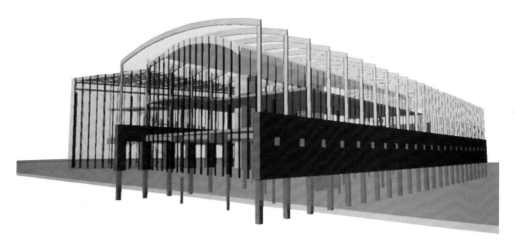

Sport and recreation are, without a doubt, an important component of civilised life, and active relaxation skills are one of the criteria of civilised development. The need to combine work skills with recreational skills calls for appropriate education in that respect.

The combination of didactic functions and sports in one building, as a result of the location, acquires a symbolic meaning. This symbiosis makes it possible, in a most natural way, to make evident the need for the co-existence of work and rest, as two inseparable components of life.

The architectural solution is an attempt at an answer to the problem of blending together historical and modern contexts. The historical context is determined by the main building of the Academy of Economics, built 100 years ago as a shelter and is also defined by the existing dormitory, similar in style to the main building, albeit erected under Socialism. The modern context is the recently developed academic building and library.

The functional layout of the structure assures independent use of the various zones. The entrance zone, provides for separate access to all respective functional areas and the students can move to lecture rooms entirely outside the zone frequented by the users of the sports halls and the swimming pool.

The academic building, planned for construction in stage two, has been designed as a three-section structure. The middle section is to house the vertical systems of transportation, service installations and storage. The two extreme sections will house administration, scientific and technical staff, and small lecture rooms/classrooms. The classroom level is linked via a communicating overhead corridor with the lecture halls in the academic pavilion. This solution creates an integrated lecture complex, despite construction in several stages.

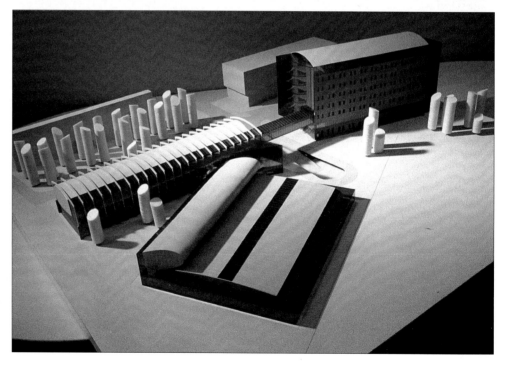

THE WANDERING HOUSE
Architectural Visions for Europe

The 'Architectural Visions for Europe' exhibition, held in Berlin's Charlottenburg Palace Orangery in 1994, invited architects to create a building harmoniously merging all major functions of urban life.

Each design team was assigned one of six consecutive lots on a commercial wharf in Düsseldorf, on the right bank of the Rhine. Each of their ten-storey buildings, based on a 15-metre-square plan with two symmetrically placed lower adjuncts, was to comprise flats, offices, recreation facilities, an elevator and a two-level underground garage.

Another requirement was that the design should be inspired by certain technologies and materials offered by the sponsoring companies – manufacturers of construction material and products. The prescribed materials were glass and steel for most of the construction, glass, steel and gypsum panels for the elevator shaft and the interiors.

Romuald Loegler presented the idea of a 'wandering' house, 'moved' into and integrated with various historic contexts, which is reflected in the form. The static, vertically oriented interior is contrasted with the slanted, glazed curtain outside, expressing the idea of movement. The flexible structural system and a minimal number of various materials create the appearance of lightness, of being liberated from gravity. The most original detail is the spherical elevator.

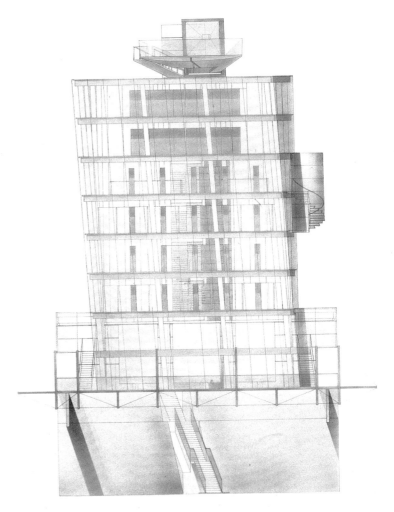

Elevations; OVERLEAF, ABOVE: Section, plan and axonometric of the spherical elevator

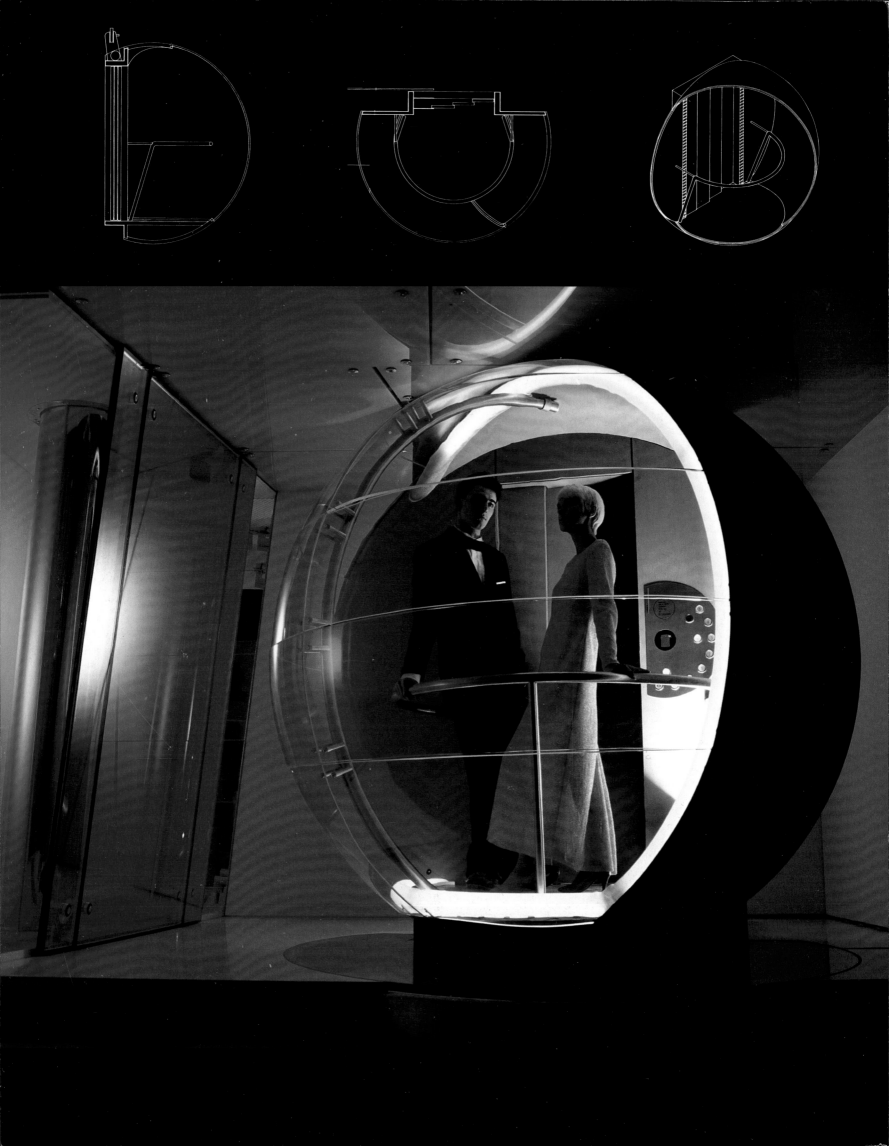